Good Mom on Paper

edited by **Stacey May Fowles** *and* **Jen Sookfong Lee**

GOOD MOM ON PAPER

Writers on Creativity and Motherhood

ESSAIS SERIES NO. 13

BOOK*HUG PRESS
TORONTO 2022

FIRST EDITION

Library and Archives Canada Cataloguing in Publication
Title: Good mom on paper : writers on motherhood and creativity / edited by Stacey May Fowles and Jen Sookfong Lee.
Names: Fowles, Stacey May, editor. | Lee, Jen Sookfong, editor.
Series: Essais (Toronto, Ont.) ; no. 13.
Description: Series statement: Essais ; no. 13
Identifiers: Canadiana (print) 20210371064 | Canadiana (ebook) 2021037117X
ISBN 9781771667470 (softcover)
ISBN 9781771667487 (EPUB)
ISBN 9781771667494 (PDF)
Subjects: LCSH: Motherhood. | LCSH: Mothers. | LCSH: Creation (Literary, artistic, etc.) | CSH:
Canadian essays (English)—21st century. | LCGFT: Essays.
Classification: LCC PS8367.M68 G66 2022 | DDC C814/.608035252—dc23

The production of this book was made possible through the generous assistance of the Canada Council for the Arts and the Ontario Arts Council. Book*hug Press also acknowledges the support of the Government of Canada through the Canada Book Fund and the Government of Ontario through the Ontario Book Publishing Tax Credit and the Ontario Book Fund.

Canada Council for the Arts Conseil des Arts du Canada
ONTARIO ARTS COUNCIL
CONSEIL DES ARTS DE L'ONTARIO
an Ontario government agency
un organisme du gouvernement de l'Ontario
Canada
ONTARIO CREATES | ONTARIO CRÉATIF

Book*hug Press acknowledges that the land on which we operate is the traditional territory of many nations, including the Mississaugas of the Credit, the Anishnabeg, the Chippewa, the Haudenosaunee, and the Wendat peoples. We recognize the enduring presence of many diverse First Nations, Inuit, and Métis peoples and are grateful for the opportunity to meet, work, and learn on this territory.

Contents

Introduction

STACEY MAY FOWLES AND JEN SOOKFONG LEE

This is a book born of frustration. Through a number of (often angry) conversations, the two of us began to articulate how we felt about our day-to-day struggles with being both mothers and writers.

For us, it felt like to excel in the business of literature you were better off hiding the fact that you had any children at all. Better to conceal the necessity of your school drop-offs and pickups, never inconvenience anyone with the reality of a kid's sick day, never admit the mad scramble for last minute child care, lest you be labelled "difficult." We shared a growing discomfort with the dominant literary culture—how it has a tendency to ignore, misunderstand, make light of, or even mock our very real experiences. In fact, when you become a mother who makes creative work, it becomes clear whom our systems are built for, and whom they are built to exclude.

Through these conversations, we started to feel like it was vital to create a project that highlighted the unique challenges and triumphs that came along with making motherhood and a creative life work. The manuscript written or artist's talk given with a baby sleeping in a carrier. Missing a book launch for a bedtime, crafting a promotional tour around child care, forgoing a radio spot for daycare drop-off. The exhaustion, the anger, the fear, the sheer impossibility of making it all happen—all while making it look like it was easy.

Yes, there was a great deal of frustration we felt needed to be articulated, but also immense gratitude—gratitude to writerly mothers who made us postpartum casseroles and gave us toddler hand-me-downs, who helped with much-needed publishing and parenting support, who gave us a shoulder to cry on in the hardest moments. *Good Mom on Paper* is grown from the knowledge that mothers are each other's most valuable resource, whether providing a safe, nonjudgmental place to complain, or a playbook on how to get things done. We wanted to pull together a collection that could offer creative mothers and mothers-to-be solace through their struggles, comfort through their fears, and a realistic picture of what it means to be passionate about our work, while taking care of the small people in our lives.

We understand that motherhood is not a monolith, and that experiences vary. This is not a book about "having it all" or being a "mom boss." Instead, it's a thoughtful collection of honest and varied reflections on how challenging, beautiful, confusing, and messy it can be to raise good people while also being good to ourselves. *Good Mom on Paper* showcases the sacrifices (there are many) and the successes (they're both small and large), and gets beyond clichés and acceptable answers to the question of what motherhood means to creators. It examines how children have the potential to both open up a whole new realm of inspiration, and to kill a career in progress. It goes deep into the conflict between fulfilling our dreams and providing support to the people we love the most. It critiques the very systems, beliefs, and institutions that make all these choices so very hard in the first place.

Every experience of motherhood is different, and we've tried to build a collection that reflects and celebrates that difference. But we also know that motherhood is a shared project, one better supported by a community of understanding than relegated to the troublesome shadows of our culture. We know that mothers are connected by a struggle to fit into structures that at best fail to nurture us, and at worst keep us out.

Good Mom on Paper is also a place to celebrate successes in a world that would often have us minimize them. Jennifer Whiteford writes of completing a novel while mothering and working during a pandemic: "(I)t is a big deal. Just like so many other things that mothers do. There are so many big deals around us that we turn into small deals. Or that the world around us turns into small deals."

After reading this finished collection, we were struck by how much comfort these stories would have brought us during those terrifying, confusing early days of motherhood; days where everything, including creativity, felt impossible. We are also struck by how much comfort they bring now, even just in knowing we were and are still not alone.

Mothers have long been telling each other these kinds of vital stories in private, and now it's time to make them available to everyone who needs them. The struggles with strollers and adolescence, disabilities and fertility, marriage and loneliness have never fit into the shadows of creative life.

Here they are, in the light.

ONE

TIME

The Dog Was Fine

CARRIE SNYDER

The dog was fine.

I want you to know that.

I am writing about an ordinary afternoon in mid-December: while shopping for Christmas presents uptown, I'd noticed a dog tied to the bike rack outside the liquor store. I know that isn't a particularly unusual sight—people do leave their dogs tied up while inside stores—but this dog was very unhappy. It was whining and pacing as best it could on its shortened leash. I could hear it whimpering from across the street.

My heart dropped down into my stomach.

I slowed my pace, looking, straining to see, in hopes that the dog's owner might appear and ease the pain in my heart. The pain spreading all through my body. Into my bones.

The pain screaming inside my head.

I heard myself groan audibly. *Oh!* I'd cried out, for anyone to hear. *Oh, I can't stand this.*

Should I cross the street and crouch down beside the dog, sit with it, try to soothe it? I wondered. But it wants its owner, not me, not a stranger.

I tried to shake it off, tried to think reasonably, rationally. I said to myself, "This dog is not your responsibility, and furthermore, you are projecting your own emotions on to the dog. You don't really know what the dog is feeling, or whether it is even suffering. You certainly don't know that it's been abandoned."

How can I explain? I kept walking, slowly, watching the dog from across the street, while the pain remained, so agonizing that it seemed like something I simply could not bear to feel. Feeling it would kill me. Seeing the dog, seeing what looked like suffering, like the suffering of abandonment, my guts turned to water. It felt like I was falling.

If this were a projection of my own emotions on to the dog's situation, did that suggest my own emotional state was intolerable? Or was I genuinely in touch with the dog's needs? What was happening here? How could I remove this painful overattachment to another creature, in order to continue on with my day, to lead a sane life?

Boundaries. Is that what I lack?

Nurses and doctors and teachers and social workers and psychologists and paramedics and anyone whose job it is to remain functional and whole while working with people who are suffering must be able to separate themselves from that suffering. They can't be porous or transparent, they can't flood with human agony, or even with human joy, or they will burn out. In fact, they can't be flooded with anything other than their own sensible responses to what they're observing and assisting with, no matter how awful or degrading or frightening.

To operate otherwise would be to drown in a vast ocean of pain, a neverending wash of grief and misery and loss and fear, feeling what it feels like to be hurt in myriad ways.

But my boundaries are like wet tissue paper, in danger of tearing, shredding at the lightest brush with someone else's experience. Perhaps I became a writer because it gave me a place to organize, manage, put to practical use these emotions that flow so freely into me, that I invite in.

I am also a mother.

The presents I was buying, so heavy on my shoulders, were books for my children. Every Christmas, alongside practical items like warm socks, gloves, and pajamas, I give my children books, so many books that the piles of wrapped rectangular packages under the tree have become a family joke: *from Mom ... now what could this be?*

I guess with books I am offering them maps of the world, of human experience. I guess I want for them what books have given to me: the flow of a phrase or memorized line from someone else's imagination into my own, that in any moment of floundering might drop down a rope and haul me out of the mire. I hope that they will find themselves seen and rescued by books, as I have been seen and rescued by books.

The dog was fine.

I promise you that, though I shouldn't, and I can't.

The worst spells in my life have been when I felt nothing: depression.

I experience depression as complete alienation from the world around me. Interactions are drained of colour: grey, flat, dull. I become unmoored from caring, do not care, cannot care. I feel worthless, empty, leaden. Despite being in situations that invite many feelings, I can't access those feelings, they're flattened. Pressed so thin they seem to have vanished.

What bothers me most during these spells is that I can fake engagement with enough facility that no one guesses what I'm not-feeling. No one seems to notice that my smile is a mask and I am an automaton speaking her lines. I know this to be an illness and not a mindset, because it doesn't matter what I do—exercise, sleep, journal, keep on keeping on—nothing changes, nothing moves. Though perhaps these simple habits help to keep me afloat. Something does.

And then, suddenly, I can feel again, and the world opens up (or I do), and I'm flooded, and weeping over the morning newspaper, tears rolling down my cheeks.

I was stopped on the sidewalk, audibly groaning, because a dog had been tied up outside a liquor store.

I was flooded. I was drowning.

If habit and routine keep me afloat during periods of not-feeling, writing seems to be a safety valve, a release from feeling too much. Writing is when—or how—I access my boundaries. In composing stories, I remove the feelings like they are treasures, delicate and special trinkets to be discovered and examined and displayed; I array them across the page, letting my characters feel and fight and try to fix themselves. I do this very calmly. I don't weep while writing even very sad scenes, though sometimes afterward I feel shaken and disturbed by what I've witnessed in my mind's eye. But it is there on the page, and I sit up straight and leave it where it lies. I exhale deeply and return to my body feeling lighter somehow. The world is sorted. It makes sense on the page in a way that it doesn't in the body, and in a way that the body doesn't in the world.

I crossed at the lights. If I kept walking, soon I wouldn't be able to see the dog anymore. It was here that I made a plan: I would text my husband, who works in an office only a block from the liquor store, and ask him to walk that way home. Then, in a few hours, I would know the fate of the dog. It would either be gone, or it would be there, and if it was there, I could spring into action, which at that point would be perfectly warranted.

The plan freed me to continue walking home to the tasks that awaited, shoulders weighed down by cloth bags filled with books for my children.

I could have wrapped the gifts when I got home, but instead, after texting my husband, I sat down, and began to write this. *I want you to know that the dog was fine*, I wrote; though in truth, even hours later, when my husband got home, I could not be absolutely certain of that fact.

There was only the absence of evidence. The dog was gone.

My compulsion to tell the truth is stronger than my compulsion to protect you from feeling pain.

I'm sorry.

This is a particular weakness of mine, and one that I'm wrestling with even as I write these words. A writer can tell the truth—she can be brutally honest with a reader; but a mother can't, not on the page. A mother protects her children. I feel this at a level so deep I hardly know how to say it out loud—it comes out of my throat in a roar.

I've never viewed my choice to be a mother as a sacrifice. I hate that word, actually—*sacrifice*—its stench of self-imposed martyrdom. But maybe this is where it comes and meets me. Where I can't be both mother and writer.

A child's story is not directed by their mother, no matter how a mother might stand in the wings and whisper the desired lines, or worse, operate strings from above. The child has to be who they are, and even if their narrative is directed or told by someone—anyone—else, they will be who they are deep inside, within their most private self. If suppressed or imposed upon, their other story, their true story, will emerge in painful glimpses, or splatters of defiance, or violent wrenching, or silent fortitude, endurance. But it won't vanish.

It's odd, but when witnessing a child's pain—my own child's, I mean—I've observed myself become like my writer self, by which I mean the self that is writing. I detach from projection, and become pure witness, observer, attuned like an animal to the needs of the other, the watched, the protected, the one who must be cared for and kept alive. I lose myself entirely. I become so porous that I'm no longer myself, but a receptive antennae. I take my commands from somewhere out there in the universe.

When a child needs me, I see as if from a neutral vantage point, where there can be no blame, because we are all caught inside our own narratives, unfolding as they must, adjacent to other narratives, but essentially uncontrollable. (That's something I shouldn't confess, especially as a fiction writer: the way a story tells itself to me, as if it already exists. The way I try out various plot ideas only to have characters refuse to enact them. I observe where a story is going, and follow it there, discovering what it's trying to tell me. I collect clues and pay attention. Oh, I pay so much attention.)

When a child needs me, my focus becomes laser sharp. Most of what I offer takes the form of a question: I aim to understand every fact, every theory, every proposal, every therapy, every option. I probe, I wonder, I ask and ask and ask. And through witnessing, observing, questioning, somehow the story unfolds in a way that seems natural and unforced, it is happening as it must. The way stories do. The way life does.

I suppose my own detachment from cause and effect is protection, in the heat of a crisis. The difficulties arise afterward, when the crisis is past. When I re-enter my body as a shambling, needy, contradictory, self-absorbed, aching, imperfect human being, the suffering of the world seems to flow directly into my bloodstream. But whose suffering is this? How can I possibly know?

When I was a new mother deep in diapers and soaked in breast milk, I felt bounteous, and it seemed that if only I could give my babies a series of homemade gentle days and months and years, a treasured existence, if only they knew they were loved, they would grow up to be happy; whatever that meant to me at the time. I'm not sure. I knew, on some level, it wasn't really entirely up to me to produce contented children; but on another level, I was damn well intent on trying.

And I applaud those efforts.

And I let them go.

In this way, I've been able to walk with my children through experiences that could have swallowed us whole. I walked, attuned to what was useful and available in me to offer them. The rest, I jettisoned.

This is not so very different from how, as an ambitious young writer, I believed that through effort I could become the writer that I aspired to be, write books like those that had rescued—that still rescue—me.

And I applaud those efforts.

And I let them go.

Here, somewhere in the muddled middle, I'm wondering where this leaves me, the writer who watches the stories unfold, who tries to see through another's eyes, and not through her own. She's written out of the story, you see, the way the writer should be. But she was there, and she was me, a mother mothering in extreme circumstances, the kind no one wants to imagine herself attending to; and I'm here to tell you that it was kind of okay. We're okay. I'm okay.

I would like very much for that to be my uncomplicated message.

But I might be fooling myself. I might be deluded. I might be a hot melting mess, who weeps over the newspaper every morning because she hasn't processed her own feelings on this subject. I might cry out at the leashed dog's whimpers because that is what my pain feels like, only it's stored somewhere I can only access when projecting it on to another suffering being.

I might not be dealing with this all as well as I'd like to believe.

I might not be okay. Okay?

Maybe someday, years from now, the feelings will be broken down into rich, fertile compost, not this raw, sharp, indigestible mass that doesn't belong on the page; not yet. Maybe then I'll discover a character who can carry these feelings off.

For now, I'm here. Feeling. And feeling is better than not feeling. So much better. Feeling something, even a level of pain so fresh it climbs out of my throat as an involuntary groan on a grey December afternoon, is so much better than feeling nothing, a flatlining of the spirit that drains experience of meaning. Feeling is full of meaning. Give me feeling any minute of any day.

I want to be unprotected. I want the world to be lit up in all colours.

I don't know what I can survive, because no one knows that. What I know is this: it is a privilege to be with someone who is suffering and who is willing to let you be with them, whether that someone is a child or a character. What a gift, to be a trusted witness, companion, seeker along the same path. A character deserves dignity (or so I believe), but they are an invention, a fiction, a container for the writer's wounds and joys, protected by reason of being not-real; safe. A child is almost entirely the opposite of what I've just described: very much real, vulnerable, containing the promise of change, renewal, contradiction, and selfness that must be preserved, protected, kept whole. To write down a child's suffering would be to pin them to the page. No! I want for them a million different possibilities, and of their own discovery.

A child is not a character.

And so I turn away from the page, despite being a writer.

The dog was fine. As are we.

I want you to know that.

That Time in Trailer #289

MEAGHAN STRIMAS

The trailer key was tied to a broom handle, cut to a two-foot stump, similar to something a gas station attendant might hand over after being asked about bathrooms. At some point, someone—maybe Chopper, maybe his wife, whom I'd never met in the two decades Chop had worked at the camp—got fed up with that key being misplaced.

Chop was proud of Trailer #289 and insisted on showing me around. We stood, shoulder to shoulder, on the scuffed white linoleum as he pointed to the mini-fridge, the hot plate, the cupboards, the table, the loveseat, the bed. He showed me how to run the blinds and work the thermostat. A big selling point was that it had AC.

"Not bad for the price, heh?"

An obvious joke, since I was getting the place for free.

My dad and Chopper were workmates at Whispering Pines camp in Hepworth, at the southernmost edge of Ontario's Bruce Peninsula. The trailer sat in a clump of trees, a five-minute walk from the Pines' main gate, right next to a playground for the campers' kids. It had been sold, sight unseen, to a new set of seasonals who weren't moving in until the following spring, and I was told that as long as I kept Chop "in his Tim's" I could use the place for a few weeks to do some writing.

Chopper, who'd earned his nickname from a wood-splitting accident that sent him flying and left him with a bad back, gave me one more word of advice before leaving: "Don't be opening the door to any old-timers, especially one with a long, white pony-hair thing."

It took me a few seconds to figure out what he meant by *pony-hair*.

"He'll chew your ear off."

"Okay, thanks."

"Fox McKelvie. Watch out for him. He'll take your whole day away."

"Got it. Thanks."

"Hangs about the laundry. Just wanting to chat, chat, chat. *Mr. Chit-Chats*—that's what your dad calls him. We got a list *yay*-long of complaints."

Chop sat on the trailer's deck stairs and lit a smoke.

"Did I tell you my daughter's writing a book, too?"

Chop's daughter is eleven.

I popped a piece of gum and sat.

I could start work a little later.

I was in this trailer because I had to finish a book, a new collection of poetry. My third. It was June 2015, and I'd agreed to hand the finished manuscript over to my friend and editor, Stuart Ross, in August. I had a few poems in a near-finished state, but not nearly enough for a collection. I had two months to write a book, which is not reasonable. I wasn't thinking. I went ahead with this ridiculous plan because I'd agreed to the deadline, not because I had any faith in what I had to say. Only young people and people who've never actually written a book buy into the romance of the writing life.

Even my own mother has said to me, "I don't know why you bother writing poetry." This makes me laugh because it's a good question: I often wonder the same thing. In my early twenties, one of my uncles, a speech writer whom I admired, mailed me a photocopy of a news story titled "Poetry Is Dead." It was a taunt that was meant to sting. I knew he'd snorted with laughter as he licked the envelope.

My approach to getting the book done was workmanlike. I had work to do. And I came prepared: a grocery-store bag full of hard-boiled eggs and books; in my purse, a pad of paper, a few pens, and a couple of sleeves of nic gum. My mom looked after my toddler at her place in Owen Sound. My husband stayed back in Toronto, recovering from cancer treatment.

The truth was, I would have rather been clocking in at a construction site. I fancied the idea of the camaraderie, of being made queasy by the sun and the roaring of machines, so loud that I couldn't hear myself think, of the possibility of three beers with lunch.

Of course, I would've been fired on my third day.

I shut the trailer door and slid the latch to "lock" before tossing the key and its wooden chaperone on the kitchenette table, where I set up a makeshift desk. The surface was sticky with drink and covered with rings from cups of Crown Royal and the good Mateus. Meat on a bun, left to rot in the heat by Chop's teenage son, had brought flies in numbers. There must have been at least one hundred dead ones crammed in the windowsills, and as I slowly opened the window closest to the table, it left a small hill of corpses.

A light breeze blew a tiny dead fly across the table and onto a sheet of paper I'd torn from my notepad.

"Hello, fly."

I was alone. Which was the idea, obviously—poetry is not a group activity. But at that time, it wasn't entirely my choice. I had already felt alone for months; I couldn't remember the last time I had shared a meal with another adult instead of pounding cupcakes in the dark while leaning against the kitchen counter. I still had Nathan, my husband, but he could no longer eat with me in the normal way, thanks to the radiation that had burnt his throat, inside and out. What nutritionists and psychologists say is true: dining with others promotes more sensible eating habits; sharing a meal, sitting down and chatting with someone you like, helps to weather the hassles of everyday life.

Nathan and I even slept and lived in separate parts of the house. We'd built our nests—his on the living room couch, and mine in our spare room. (I couldn't bear to sleep in the bed we normally shared.)

It had been a shit winter. My whole life had become about getting through each day without being found out. Hustling the baby to daycare in the dark, I was always worried about being late for work.

A decade earlier, my solution for a traumatic time would have involved endless cigarettes, endless bottles of sparkling white wine, and endless nights out with friends. But I could not do that now. I was a mom.

Motherhood, writing, and suffering: each a lonely business.

I gave birth to Lou on the top floor of Toronto's St. Michael's Hospital, just under a year before my time in Trailer #289, with Nathan holding my hand and my mother nearby, texting updates to my sisters. ("Melisa wants to know how much you're dilated, honey.") Lou was born hours earlier than any of the nurses had predicted. When I sent my mother to get help, certain the baby was on his way, she'd discovered the nurse casually spinning in her chair at the station. The baby was almost out before they even entered the room.

The first weeks and months of new motherhood crawled by. I loved my baby, but I wasn't so sure that I loved my new life. The people who knew me best were proud of me because I seemed to be doing such a good job. A few even admitted they were surprised at how well I had adjusted. They were shocked that the same woman who—up until her mid thirties, claimed she'd never have a baby, and who never, ever left a bar before last call—had learned how to tie a Maman Kangourou baby wrap. And I *was* adjusting—so much so that, after a while, I did not even twitch when the woman who ran Baby Music Hour at the local rec centre asked, "And how's Baby today, Mom?"

(I wasn't completely new to parenthood when I had Lou. I'd been a stepmom of two children for five years before that, so I was familiar with doing things that would have previously felt ridiculous—like laying out an outfit, called "a person," every school night so my stepdaughter wouldn't get anxious trying to decide what to wear in the morning.)

What no one knew was how angry I was with myself: I could see the before and the after. I could see how luxurious my life had been pre-motherhood, and how much time I had then that I was barely aware of, and that was now utterly gone.

I was angry, too, that I was not writing. I'd already published a couple of books of poems, but like most such collections, they went largely unnoticed. I was at a crossroads in terms of my identity as a writer even before getting pregnant. And then, like it does for so many women, new motherhood doused my creative aspirations. Those aspirations sat in a glass jar on the shelf, right beside the Baby Mum-Mums and creamed green beans.

I'd been warned that having a child would make writing feel inconvenient, irrelevant, and self-indulgent, so I wasn't very surprised when this is exactly what happened. I had also heard of mothers who would work while the baby naps, but that just mystified me: while my baby slept, I searched the internet for items that might help him sleep better and longer.

When Lou was a year old, I went back to a busy teaching job, having been hired full-time at a college just weeks before he was born. (I sweated my way through a series of increasingly intense interviews and mock-teaching exercises for the position while wearing ever-more loose-fitting clothing to hide my growing baby bulge. "Off to a roaring start," a gal pal had said when I told her that I had both landed the job and was pregnant.)

I wasn't exactly welcomed by some of the individuals at the college who liked to refer to themselves as "senior faculty." I'd never gone to teachers' college, and unlike the two women who had been hired the same time as me, I did not have a PhD, nor any interest in acquiring one. And, of course, I'd spent my first year as a full-time professor on unpaid mat leave. And it quickly became obvious that my creative aspirations and meagre successes as a writer did not inspire awe among my peers.

Plus, I was a *mother*. A new one.

Gross.

I was still breastfeeding—my tits were heavy and huge. At work, they ached for my son. My right breast, the one I'd named Bessy, after a cow my mom had been most fond of as a child, would spurt milk if I accidently brushed up against the edge of my desk. She was a prize milker *and* the cause of great stress. I often wished I could leave her at home.

One of my colleagues shouted, "Babies, yuck!" when I mentioned I'd had a hard time leaving my one-year-old son at daycare that morning. None of the three women I shared an office with had children. In their view, I was an unethical, selfish idiot because I'd brought a child into this godawful world.

I was a writer, a mother, and a professor—to borrow a great Alice Munro title: who did I think I was?

Three months after my return to work, my husband got diagnosed with throat cancer. He immediately began a rigorous course of radiation and chemo, and our lives became about coping. As irrational and immature as it sounds, I felt like I'd been abandoned by him to care for our son on my own. (The reality was that he was fighting to survive.)

One morning, after dropping Lou off so I could drive the hour to work, I screamed at the windshield the entire way. I was so hoarse that I could barely teach my classes.

I did, though.

Sometimes, I'd hide in a bathroom so I could breathe for a few minutes. I had my favourite stall, and it was there, in this grubby cubicle, that I sat and sobbed after a student said she could tell I was trying, but that she was sick of being taught by people like me, people with "fairytale lives." I was tempted to tell her just how wrong she was, using the two bottles of cheap white wine I'd drank the night before as evidence.

Loser, loser, loser, I chanted as I hit the side of my head with my fist, again and again.

Around this time, my friend Stuart called to see how I was doing. His wife Laurie had recently completed cancer treatment, so Stu understood much of what I was going through.

I confessed that I was falling apart.

He suggested I write something, and said that if I wrote a new book of poems, he'd edit it and publish it under his poetry imprint. My first impulse was to say *no*. There was no way I could write a book in the middle of all this mess.

I said *yes*.

I did my two weeks in Trailer #289 and I finished the book, *Yes or Nope*. The AC kept me cool and helped drown out the whining of the chainsaws and leaf blowers. The old timer with the pony-hair never came by. I read and I wrote and I napped in the sun, curled up in the loveseat because I was too afraid to stretch out on the bed. (The soiled mattress looked like an ancient map that had been rescued from a mouldy trunk.) The flies stayed until I was ready to leave. I left the place spotless. A small gesture of thanks.

The book received some very positive reviews, got added to a couple of course lists, and won an award. Writing, I was relieved to discover, still held a significant place in my life.

The night I won the award, I celebrated with Nathan and Stu at a nearby bar. My parents had, as usual, offered to babysit, and even drove down from Owen Sound to do so. At some point, someone suggested I take a break from the white wine after the guys tending bar started calling me *Miss Chardonnay*. Getting up to use to the bathroom, I stumbled against a chair, and Nathan called out, in the voice of a corner store lotto ticket machine: "*Winner! Gagnant!*"

When we got home that night, my dad asked what I was going to do with all the money. (I declined to tell him that it would all go against our credit card debt.) I crossed that hall and stood over my baby's crib and watched him as he slept. This was my life. What had I done to deserve all of this?

Recently, Lou made a card for Nathan and me that said, "I love you because you help me when I am struggling." We laughed because we'd never heard him speak of any struggles. Has he ever really had any? One morning, while I was bending over to put on my socks, still partially undressed, Lou said, "Mommy, your boobies look like two hanging bats."

"Thanks a lot, Lou."

"What? I love bats," he said.

The narrator of Sigrid Nunez's novel *What Are You Going Through* says, "There are two kinds of people in the world: Those who upon seeing someone else suffering think, That could happen to me, and those who think, That will never happen to me. The first kind of people help us to endure, the second kind make life hell." Children help us get through—maybe not actively or wittingly, but they do. Sometimes they keep us alive because they need us to keep *them* alive. They are tied to us like hunks of wood to a key, and we are duty-bound to preserve them.

Kids also force us to get out of our own little heads. They keep us so busy that we don't have time to feel sorry for ourselves. I have a friend who says that as the childfree get older, their worlds get smaller and smaller. It's a terrible thing to say, and I don't know that I'm convinced. But I can say that being a mom has made me less self-involved, less self-absorbed, which means I'm also kinder, easier to be around.

It's been five years since I wrote the book that won the award. I've picked away at a new book of poems, plus some stories that never get too far. I work hard at being a good mom. But it seems that, when it comes to writing, I'm still at the same crossroads, assaulted by the same unanswerable question of *why bother*. (Even writing this essay, which I forced myself to do because I needed to prove to myself that I could—and because my husband and a few writer friends prodded me—brought up those familiar feelings of guilt.)

Sometimes I worry that it will take another crisis, another painful and unhinged time, for me to write in any kind of focused way again, to carve out the space, give myself the permission to sit at a small kitchenette table, alone and engrossed in the process, for days on end.

Sometimes I think I'd give my right tit, the milky one, for another two weeks in Trailer #289.

That Kind of Mother

JAEL RICHARDSON

The first time I faced a day alone with my newborn son, I was terrified.

It wasn't the typical new-mom-fear, the kind that's rooted in worry for the safety and well-being of a fresh and fragile life. I was not worried about letting him sleep in his own crib. I wasn't uncertain about my ability to calm him if he cried. My fear was far more inward in focus.

I was thinking about what was going to become of my days now that I had a baby with needs that conflicted with my own. I was thinking about all of the work and the writing that would never get done with quite the same ease. I was wondering how I would accomplish all the goals and plans I had laid out for myself that required quiet focus.

I like to know what's coming. I like to be prepared. It suits me well in my day job as a festival director, where planning and scheduling are critical. But on that first day, I knew that nothing would be straightforward or predictable about life with a newborn.

Would I get time to write?

Would I get enough sleep?

Should I clean while he naps, or should I mark papers?

These were the thoughts that piled up, one on top of the other, as I sat in the nursery, feeding my son, alone together for the first time. *What do I do now?*

Most of the people I knew who had newborns told nightmare stories of sleepless nights and hectic days. Of getting nothing done for months, years, even. It was normal. A rite of passage.

"That's parenting."

"You'll be fine. Eventually."

"Just enjoy every minute," they told me.

But I was in graduate school. I had not taken the semester off to have a baby, despite my professor's advice. Getting nothing done and not getting any sleep were not viable options. I needed a new plan that worked for me.

So, when a friend told me about a book with a strategy and routine she had used to teach her daughter to sleep through the night by the time she was six weeks old, I bought it. Doing nothing—simply hoping for moments of productivity—was too stressful.

The book was small and thin, and when it arrived in the mail, I read it cover to cover. *Train your child in the way you want them to go*, the book said, an allusion to a verse in the Bible. *Teach them the difference between daytime and nighttime from the start.*

So, I did. I taught my son the difference between day naps and nighttime sleep just like the book described. I fed him and put him down for naps on a schedule. I was vigilant, using his long, predictable naps to write and mark. Within six weeks, he was sleeping through the night, and I was getting things done. The house fell into a new routine, and finally motherhood felt manageable.

When the Ontario government announced in March 2020 that kids would be staying home and learning online because of a global pandemic, I felt the same way I did that first time I was home alone with my son. I panicked. *What do I do now? How will I get it all done?*

My son was eleven, and I was no longer in school, no longer marking. Now, I ran a charitable organization from home. I had staff and a board of directors to report to. In addition to my full-time job, I was writing a novel and doing biweekly book reviews on the radio—activities I often worked on in the evenings and on weekends, especially while my son was at basketball practice.

When the work got too busy, when the deadlines piled up or when festival planning became overwhelming, I sent my son to spend time with my siblings. He loved family sleepovers, and there were plenty of cousins nearby to choose from.

But in lockdown, there were no sleepovers and no practices, and the prospect of being at home indefinitely with all the same deadlines and none of these supports worried me.

Now, it was just my husband, my son, and me. Just the three of us.

In the first week of online learning, his school assigned hours of work each day. Assignment after assignment to complete on various online platforms. *Read this story and answer these questions. Film a video of yourself. Use this app to make a presentation.*

But I was feverishly trying to convert plans for an in-person festival into a virtual one, while also completing the final edits for my debut novel, eight years in the making.

I struggled to get anything done. I had difficulty focusing and completing basic tasks. Reading, a pastime I had always enjoyed, suddenly felt taxing.

"I've got a meeting, so finish your math, do your reading, and I'll check in when I'm done," I would say. But whenever I left him to figure out his schoolwork alone, there were tantrums of frustration.

"I can't do it."

"I don't understand."

"I'm not good at this."

I worried that the challenges of lockdown life and independent learning were too much. He was a social kid with no other children in the house. He was bored and he missed his friends and teammates. I missed how happy he was joking with his classmates and competing on the basketball court.

"I'm not an only child. I'm a lonely child," he said one day, and my heart ached with guilt.

I decided that the most effective way to support him was to become his teaching assistant and classmate—setting my own work aside to sit with him during the school day, willing to help him whenever he wanted. He would get all of my focus, so he wouldn't feel so alone.

Maybe this was some existential way of creating personal growth, of adjusting my attention. Work isn't everything, after all. Maybe I just needed to set new priorities. Maybe I needed to become that devoted, my-kid-is-the-centre-of-my-world kind of mother—the kind of mother I had always admired.

So, I woke up early and did a few hours of uninterrupted festival planning work before his school day started, pushing my meetings later in the day in order to help him through his assignments. When his schooling began, I sat with him all day before returning to my own work. I listened to audiobooks while I cooked dinner and cleaned the house, and I worked on the novel late at night, exercising whenever and wherever I could manage.

As the weeks went on, the exhaustion of trying to schedule too much into each day mounted. Sure, I was getting things done. But I was tired and miserable. I was short-tempered and irritable.

"Why am I the only one who puts the dishes in the dishwasher?"

"How can you put a ball in a hoop but you can't put clothes in a basket?"

"Why am I the only one who can see that there's pee on the toilet?"

To ensure I got as much work done as possible and to relieve some of the strain, after school and on weekends, we let him use the PlayStation. Before the pandemic, between weekday limitations, basketball practice and weekend tournaments, his access to video games had been limited.

In lockdown, the only routine he had was a few hours a day of online learning, so the time he spent playing video games became the most predictable and productive part of my day. He would play and chat with friends on his headset for hours without needing anything. Within weeks, he was gaming for up to six hours a day.

"Why do I have to get off now?" he would say at 9:00 p.m.

"Because it's bedtime, and you've played long enough."

"Just one more game."

"If you're not up in ten seconds, you won't get on tomorrow."

And while this threat often worked, it always felt hollow when I said it. I didn't want to take away the PlayStation. I needed it as much as he did. I just wanted him to obey.

So, in addition to the unpredictable chaos of at-home learning and the exhaustion of an impossible routine, there was guilt. Guilt from having every luxury and still struggling to find the right balance. Guilt from letting my son play video games while I worked and did the things I wanted or needed to do for my career. Guilt from not being the kind of mother I always thought I'd become.

When I got pregnant with my son after years of trying, I assumed I would be that good Pinterest mother—the kind who baked something from scratch for his birthday, who would do anything he asked. Play with me. Shoot hoops with me. Read with me. Yes, yes, absolutely, let's go. I thought that's what happened to a woman who finally had a child after waiting so long to be a mother.

But my career goals didn't change after my son was born. The things I wanted in my job felt equally important, maybe more so, and when I realized I couldn't have more children, it felt justified. This was what I was meant to be doing—not just mothering but working, writing books, and changing the publishing industry.

But this was not the kind of mothering I saw growing up. My mother had been a stay-at-home mom. My sister and most of the women in my life did not go back to work early. They did not send their kids to preschool. Whenever they were apart from their kids for work, they felt remorse or regret because they loved being home with their children.

When I dropped my son off at preschool, I wrote for six hours, and when I picked him up in the afternoon, he was smiling. He was proud to have teachers and friends, and I felt so grateful for the time and the support—for the experts who sang to him and read to him and for the kids who played with him while I worked.

"This is my coat. These are my boots. This is my friend. We had pizza," he said as he showed me around his new school on our way to the car, and I listened to every word, delighted.

My son's preschool was where I first understood what I needed as a mother—a carefully orchestrated balance of work and mothering responsibilities.

While there was guilt at the start—shame at not being the mother I had imagined I'd become—the balance I experienced from enrolling my son in preschool made me feel whole despite the lack of homecooked meals and baked goods in our house. Maybe I was not the mother I had planned to be, but perhaps it was okay to be this kind of mother as well.

In 2020, I was forced to face those fears I had felt when I was left alone with my newborn for the second time in my life. Only this time, there was no book to follow, no place to send him when life got out of balance.

Lockdown reminded me that the balance I had created in my life—my ability to build a career and mother in a way that felt good—was reliant on so many other people in my community: teachers, coaches, family members, neighbours, and friends—people who made room for me to do the things I love by helping me raise my son.

I had become the kind of mother I needed to be because of the support I received from others, and when much of that disappeared as a result of a global pandemic, I could not hold it together. I struggled in every way.

Birth at the End of the World

SOFIA MOSTAGHIMI

I used to say that I believed in small pleasures. Leaning an arm outside a streetcar window on a hot summer day. Stretching the tip of a drinking straw open, hearing that crack. Slipping warm legs underneath cool sheets at night. Wedging that final piece of a puzzle into its neighbouring grooves. Listening, sleepily, to the tapping of fresh morning rain.

I used to say that I believed in beauty. The struggle for justice. That even one life changed meant something.

Now, I'm not so sure any of it matters anymore. I cry a lot. In those tears, I count my blessings, and as I do, I feel guilty. *You are one of the lucky ones*, a voice inside me says. *People have so much less than you.* But why should the fact that some have so much less put me at ease? The injustice makes everything worse.

I am seven months pregnant, and I wonder how I can be a mother—or a writer—if I haven't got any hope.

Three months into my pregnancy, my house caught fire. I haven't been home in a long time, because I haven't got one to go to. My partner J and I have been displaced into temporary housing until our home becomes liveable again.

Pregnancy is typically a time of optimism. I know that. But there is a pandemic quietly raging outside. Lockdowns and stay-at-home orders are funnelling our desperate, scattered energy into our lonely phones as we scroll through the news, watching how disproportionately this virus is killing the poor and people of colour. Important protests are happening, championing the rights of Black lives, calling awareness to the inequalities on which our racist, capitalist society is founded. A call for change that, in this increasingly polarized world, seems to go unheard.

It's the guilt that is relentless—to bring a child into *this* world, to feel such hopelessness when *she* is inside of me, brimming with new life.

And so I've been thinking a lot about the apocalypse. In fact, apocalyptic stories are the only ones that I can stand to read or think about. This may seem strange, that I'm choosing to surround myself with the darkest, most dismal stories that I can find, stories in which sad, broken characters shuffle through nightmarish dystopian landscapes in search of safety, food, and shelter. But I can relate to the surrealism of their lives, their uprootedness and powerlessness.

In the three months since the fire, I've lived in four different places. First, my sister's apartment on the second floor of an old mansion in Parkdale—filled to the brim with boxes as she prepared for a move. Then, a large, impersonal condo with a view of Lake Ontario. Then another condo, across from the CN Tower, with perpetually broken elevators and mirrors on every closet door. Finally, the first floor of an old house, badly lit with creaking hardwood floors and quaint white radiators, in walking distance of High Park. During each of these stays, I've tried to hurry along our return home by navigating a supposed system of insurance companies, contractors, and a condo corporation to whom I don't seem to matter at all.

I know this is not apocalyptic by any means. The house will be repaired. The baby will be born. My belly will deflate, slink back against the organs of my body.

Still, the irony of having become a home to my daughter just as my own was taken by fire is not lost on me.

An apocalypse is defined as destruction on a catastrophic scale, or even the total annihilation of the world. The word is derived from the Greek words *apo-* (un-) and *kaluptein* (to cover). Together, they mean to uncover, or reveal.

When there is nothing left, when all has been undone, what remains? This is what interests me about apocalyptic stories. Most tend to fall into the former catastrophic destruction definition—grave damage to societies without final obliteration. They are *post*-apocalyptic, meaning they begin during, or just after the end. These new worlds are often devoid of any organizing systems or advanced technology. They are dangerous places, without the structure we've spent thousands of years anxiously building to protect ourselves against the natural world and its many uncertainties. Food must be found. Safety must be secured against viruses, zombies, the cold, or other survivors. A post-apocalyptic world seems to quintessentially embody powerlessness.

Just as I've had no choice in my displacement due to the fire, these characters, too, must simply submit to the chaos.

Years ago, I wrote a post-apocalyptic story called "The Polluted," about a man who believes that the propagation of the human race should be staunched. To a small group of followers, he preaches that people are stains on the Earth and that overpopulation is the reason for climate change and their misery. The only way to heal the planet is to rid it of the thing that has made it sick. But one of his followers is sixteen years old. She falls in love.

It's a story that I've been returning to lately, in part because I feel I could have better executed it, and in part because these questions, of morality and procreation, still fascinate me. I want to go back to it, expand this universe, but since the fire, it's become harder for me to write. Mostly, I avoid writing. What fiction asks of the writer is for them to make choices, over and over again. Each sentence offers a thousand forked roads. My mind races. To pick one road demands a willingness to just let the others go, to stop looking back, and to give up control, with the hope that something good will come of surrendering. But I can't seem to do that right now.

Too many things could go wrong.

Inside of me, my fiction is safe. It is like the perfectly controlled and curated images of designer nurseries I scroll through on Pinterest. Since the fire, I find myself increasingly elated by time spent on this app. I search things like "small living space ideas" and "nursery polka dots." I collect images and ideas, versions of a home life that are surely unattainable. I scan baby websites, pluck items to add to an ever-growing registry. I call my mother to discuss curtains, wall colours, and bedsheets.

J was teasing me one evening. He said that my sudden urge to online shop was no surprise; that I was entering advertising's key demographic, and its most profitable: mothers. We hold the purse strings. Because, like the scavengers our foremothers were before us, we are in charge of the gathering, the consuming, the filling of the house with things.

I laughed him off, told him to be quiet.

But there is safety, and a sense of control, in the accumulation of things, isn't there? In the many post-apocalyptic stories that I have been reading, characters must spend their days scavenging abandoned homes, grocery stores, and gas stations for clothes and food.

Another irony emerges then, that accumulating things has never been more important as when capitalism has fallen.

To create is an act of hope. When I begin a story, it's because I believe that this story can be good and meaningful. If I continue to chip away at it, day after day, despite all of life's distractions, it's because I haven't lost sight of that hope. Similarly, if I conceive a child with the man I love, it's because I believe that the three of us can be happy together.

To create, then, is to believe.

This belief, however, is by no means static or uniform throughout the creative process. With hope comes a whole slew of other emotions. Doubt, dread, and fear.

Nearly three years ago, J and I brought home a kitten. It had been a dark time for me, with the cancer of a close friend, followed by the death of an aunt. But then, this little kitten appeared—so full of life, so in the present moment. I fell in love and dreamt of him every single night of the first year of his life with us. (This is not an exaggeration.) In these dreams, he would be viciously taken from me, and I would have to go and rescue him. Sometimes, in his ignorant skittishness, he had run off. Sometimes we were all in some incredible danger, due to a flood or an earthquake, and shelter needed to be found quickly.

When the time actually came for me to save my cat, I did.

Upstairs was on fire. J wanted to try and put it out. He could not be swayed otherwise. I too felt that a switch had been flipped inside of me. My movements were automatic, rehearsed through countless nights of dreaming. I found the carrier. I found the cat. I put the cat in the carrier. I screamed for J to come down. I screamed but did not go upstairs. I stayed with the cat.

When I tell people this story, jokes are made about my being psychic. I laugh along. But being psychic would imply that I had some knowledge of what was to come. I didn't. All I knew was that I had been entrusted to protect this little cat. It's why my dreams were filled with the dread of one day having to do so. It's why I felt the need to rehearse countless scenarios in my head at night while I slept.

I imagine these fears aren't so different from what will happen when she is born. In hoping that no harm will ever come to her, the many unknowns will unravel before me like a rug that leads to Hell.

It's probably why I can't stand to write any fiction right now.

In hoping too hard, we start to feel powerless, and this powerlessness feels a lot like hopelessness. It makes me wonder how much of a sense of power and control is necessary in our lives to allow for hope. On that first night after the fire, I couldn't sleep. I didn't want to forget the fear and intensity of what I felt. I wanted to hold on to it, as if holding on to it could prevent it from ever happening again.

A flash: Being awoken by a man screaming *fire* in the parking lot outside our townhome.

Another: Waking J from the couch, where he'd fallen asleep watching WWE, the TV still glaring with cartoonish feats of shiny violence. Me asking him to go look outside, with the certainty that whatever disaster was unfolding, it must be happening to someone else.

Another: *Seeing* the flames, *hearing* them as they burned ten feet high against a black, starless sky. My mind racing with possibilities.

Then the realization that this is the safest I will ever be able to keep my baby, when she is tucked away inside me.

So, which is it then? Am I meant to just let go and hope for the best? Or do I try harder to protect and prepare?

My fascination with the end of the world is not new. Most likely, it stems from an early girlhood obsession with *Buffy the Vampire Slayer*, which, at the age of twenty-five, I chose to immortalize by having the letter *B* tattooed on my right flank after downing a bottle of red wine.

(No regrets, by the way.) Up until recently, I always believed that I liked these stories because they were about controlling my fears and anxieties. I still think that's part of it. This idea that if I could consume enough of these stories, if the time came for me to experience such a catastrophe, I would be prepared. Yet the stories themselves actually embody so much powerlessness. If our characters want to remain sane, for instance, they cannot think too far ahead in time. They must take it day by day. It's the only way. To envision too far ahead is to imagine a thousand deaths.

I feel that way lately, too. Like these characters who trudge forward, I need to stay in the now.

Of course, not all characters in post-apocalyptic stories choose to go on. But I'm not interested in them. I'm interested in the ones who, in spite of such surrounding despair, do. How, and where do these characters find meaning?

In Emily St. John Mandel's *Station Eleven*, it is ten years after a deadly pandemic that has wiped out most of humanity. In Ling Ma's *Severance*, an obstinate and solitary young woman continues to go to work as a Bible product coordinator while her city, and the world around her, are decimated by a strange disease. In both, we find the act of creation to be vital to our main characters. In *Station Eleven*, a group of travelling actors and musicians perform Shakespeare plays to enclaves of survivors. In *Severance*, as New York City empties itself of life, our narrator snaps photographs of this morbid stillness, posts them up onto a blog for as long as the internet still stands.

In the first book, our characters are trading the safety of a stationary life for the nomadic life of troubadours. They sacrifice personal safety in the name of poetry. This is either very honourable, or very stupid, depending. In the second, our narrator's work demands she be a recluse. Her photographs are haunting precisely because there is no one left in New York City. That she shares these photographs online is key, just as it is important to note that the characters in *Station Eleven* perform for audiences. In both stories the thing that is giving the characters hope and meaning is the creation of slices of beauty in an otherwise ugly world. It's art, but it's also connection.

In Megan Hunter's *The End We Start From*, an unnamed narrator gives birth to a baby boy just as a terrible flood sweeps through her city, destroying her home and triggering a war. In Cormac McCarthy's *The Road*, a father and his young son travel south on a desolate and ashen American landscape. In both these stories, the parent plays the role of the protector. They must be vigilant to the world around them, to the particular ways in which they and their child could be harmed by it.

In *The Road*, the boy has never known another world, and of all the stories I've read, this is the bleakest one of all. Nearly everyone has died. Ash falls like snow from the sky. The man spends gruelling days on the road, worrying about his boy. He worries about finding him enough food, about the biting cold, about their clothes and shoes. He worries about encountering the "bad guys," of them killing the boy, or worse. He worries, too, about how hardened this way of life has made his son. He worries about all of the joyful things his son will never get to experience.

In *The End We Start From*, inside of a refugee camp, as our narrator trudges through her days, she pays close attention to her son: to how his mouth latches on to her nipple, to the particular aura of his cries at night, and to the way he learns to ball up his fist to hold tightly on to a doll made of cloth. It's the smallness of these moments that spark a feeling of beauty. It's her careful attentiveness in these moments that seem to ignite her hope.

In *The Road*, in a ransacked grocery store, the father finds a single can of Coca-Cola in an old vending machine. He gives it to the boy and tells him to drink all of it, then watches with wonder and joy as he does. Then on the southern coast, they happen upon the ocean. It's grey and ashen, like everything else. They're disappointed, and yet the father insists that the boy go swimming anyway. He rushes into the waves, and there is beauty in this, too. Here, it is the father who tries to ignite hope in his son.

There is a scene in *The End We Start From* in which the narrator asks her husband whether or not he would still have done it, had a baby with her, if he had known what was to come. We are led to believe that the husband's silence means that he does regret the baby. Maybe he doesn't regret it, and for this he is ashamed.

In *The Road*, there is the sense that the boy's mother regretted it all—the baby, her life. She commits suicide long before we've joined the travelling father and son. But when the father looks at his son, he thinks that he is feeling or knowing something about beauty and innocence.

In both, the parent goes on because they've been tasked with the protection of their child. This is enough, but it is not hope.

I suppose we might construe the baby and the boy to be signs of hope. But I've always been wary of putting that job on to children.

Despite the fire that has displaced me, it's important for me to still recognize my privilege. I have a steady job that comes with steady money, and I've been able to keep this job despite a pandemic. I have a home that is my own, with insurance to cover costs in the meantime. I am white-passing; a cisgender woman. I know, too, that only in my privilege can one be fascinated with post-apocalyptic stories. Many Black and Indigenous communities live in racist, embittered post-apocalyptic worlds already, rife with injustice. Overseas, wars continue to rage. Thousands of lives burned and blown up.

My trauma pales in comparison to that of others. But it's profound to me. In the aftermath of that night, in these feelings I felt blooming, I saw similar, terrifying moments in time, moments in which others were not so lucky as me, people who lost their homes completely, or worst, loved ones. I have felt their terror.

This is perhaps why it was so easy for me to lose hope, to put away my writing, and to proclaim that nothing really matters anyway. But it's also precisely because of this privilege that it's been necessary for me to recoup my hope. Because I survived. Because I am having a daughter in a few months' time.

Because I am a writer, and a writer's work is hope.

In a post-apocalyptic story, when all is undone and stripped of distraction, the essential questions we may otherwise ignore become the only ones that matter: What is the purpose of living? What does it mean to be human? If all hope is lost, why go on?

But in all of these stories, hope is never actually lost. I guess that's the point. It's found in human connection and beauty. It really is that simple.

Maslow's hierarchy of needs would tell us that we shouldn't care about a poem if we are starving, but these stories suggest that we won't care that we are starving if we can't find poetry in our lives. In *The Road*, the boy complains of nightmares. His father tells him that so long as he continues to have bad dreams, there is hope. It's the good dreams that we've got to be wary of. They're signs of having given up. So maybe, just maybe, my reading or writing about the end of the world is aspirational—a blueprint for hope.

To begin a story is to hope. It is to observe and to nudge, to make choices, and to accept that we don't quite know where each individual choice will lead. I never know how a story will end when it begins.

I must maintain hope that each choice will lead me to an ending that is good and meaningful.

I must trust that no matter where I end up, I will make it work.

When she is born, it will be February or March, the tail end of a long pandemic winter. It may be snowy and cold, or sunny and warm. She may come early in the morning, to the dripping sounds of melting snow, or late at night, in a rushed and hazy panic. She may be born small and sprightly, or fat and ruddy. With a full head of hair, or bald as her bum. She may cry and cry, existentially, or be a quiet and curious baby, wanting to soak up as much of the world with her eyes as she can. It's impossible to know exactly.

This is exciting but it is also terrifying. Inside of me, she is safe. However illusory, now I maintain a sense of control over her safety. After she is born, she will have the world to contend with, and it can be a cruel and unpredictable place. I won't deny her the facts of it: climate change, a mass extinction underway, the callous brutality of a capitalist system that thrives on social inequalities, white privilege's violence upon our society. I could go on. But I've caught glimpses of hope in the darkest of places. Even inside of these post-apocalyptic stories, there is joy and beauty to be found.

To see it though, I've had to let go, at least a little bit, of this overwhelming desire to try and control the world around me.

She'll have to do the same, because to be born, that's an apocalypse, too.

A Book Is Not a Baby

Why the Childbirth-Creativity Metaphor Is a Trap

RACHEL GIESE

On the day my book was published, I was lovingly deluged with Facebook messages, cards, and a bouquet of flowers bearing good wishes. "Happy Book Birthday," cheered many of those notes, as I have, in turn, cheered others; imagining a book released into the publishing marketplace, like a slippery infant making its messy way from the womb into the world.

As gestations go, my book's was long overdue. It dragged on nearly four years—three times the length of a human pregnancy and twice that of an elephant—and spanned a uniquely terrible time. Soon after I signed a deal with a publisher and began my research in earnest, I lost my full-time job, when the magazine where I worked went under. Then, three years later, while revising my final draft, my mother died suddenly in an accident.

I wrote my book—or often *didn't* write it—on a stool at my kitchen counter, watching the stove's digital clock mark the minutes that seemed to simultaneously drag and speed by. Each day began carefully divided into three parts: paid work; the current elusive chapter I was wrangling; and care for my then preteen son, who was thrashing an unhappy path through middle school. But by noon, my plans were routinely upended. A call from my son's principal about a fight at school (a frequent occurrence) meant cancelling an interview or abandoning project mid-paragraph so I could fetch my tearful child; duelling deadlines meant I was perpetually behind on one project or another; every email I sent began with the words "I'm sorry."

In the weeks following my mother's death, I developed panic attacks; hot, heart-thudding, lung-constricting surges of terror. Once, shopping for groceries at an unfamiliar store near the arena where my son practiced hockey—maternal multitasking!—I looped the outer borders of the produce section, sensing that everyone was staring at me. Flushed and panicky, I wished I could peel myself out of my skin, like a snake, and escape. I abandoned my half-full cart and waited out my son's practice in my freezing car.

The next day, I reached out to a therapist recommended by a friend. Sitting in her office in a chair by the window, with a view over a parking lot covered in March-grey slush, I spilled out my story and wept. For my mother. For me. For my son. For my faltering book. At the end of our fifty minutes, the therapist advised weekly sessions and gave me her home number, "just in case."

The summer came, then fall. I grew less furious and anxious. My son moved to a different school. With the no-nonsense guidance of an angelic copy editor, the book was finished just under the wire. The following spring, I wore a sunrise-pink suit to my book launch, while my wife wore complementary navy blue. A friend interviewed me on a stage and I was enveloped into dozens of hugs. Old friends showed up from out of town and I signed a stack of books. Afterward, there were pitchers of beer and platters of nachos in a pub, and more flowers and cards.

Happy book birthday to me! I ate it all up with a mixture of joy and grief, and a powerful sense of relief that it was over.

Despite all the book birthday wishes, launching my book didn't really feel like a birth, or a beginning, at all. I hadn't bled or torn any tender parts. I hadn't been handed a helpless bundle that I would need to feed and toilet train and nurse through ear infections and teach to drive and lose sleep over for eighteen years. If I had to employ a parental metaphor, it was more like the nest was finally emptied. But, really, more than anything, as I watched my son schmoozing with our friends and family, sucking back his too-many-th Coke, and gaming with his cousins on their phones, I recognized that writing a book was nothing like parenting. And yet, throughout Western history, from the ancients to today, creative work has, over and over and over again, been described through the metaphor of giving birth.

Men have been especially prone to this—mostly, perhaps, because, until relatively recently, women, particularly racialized and poor women, have been largely excluded from officially recognized creative work. Birth metaphors were used by Enlightenment writers and the Romantics, from Alexander Pope to Percy Bysshe Shelley ("[A] great statue or picture grows under the power of the artist as a child in the mother's womb," he writes in "A Defense of Poetry"). In 1912, James Joyce wrote in a letter to his wife, Nora, "I went then into the backroom of the office and sitting at the table, thinking of the book I had written, the child which I have carried for years and years in the womb of the imagination as you carried in your womb the children you love."

While pervasive, this analogizing hasn't been much interrogated. Back in 1991, scholar Susan Stanford Friedman captured this phenomenon in her essay "Creativity and the Childbirth Metaphor." Friedman considers what it means to liken creative work to childbirth, and how this comparison exposes, as she observes, "the structures of patriarchy that have divided labor into men's *production* and women's *reproduction*." Just as significantly, Friedman notes that this framework implies this division of labour, and of gender, can never be reconciled.

And here, let me reiterate my own guilt. I have wished many a person of many a gender a "Happy Book Birthday." Creating a narrative to contain, or even aggrandize, the creative process—to imagine it as birth or battle or marathon—can be a useful tool to push through the stretches of boredom, self-doubt, writer's block, and failure. Still, digging at this seemingly harmless construction reveals how it might not be as useful as we imagine. Why do we compare writing books to giving birth to babies, when they are really nothing like the other at all?

I'm not an expert on childbirth. I've never been pregnant, nor has my wife. My body resolutely refused to conceive. In high school and university, when I still had sex with men, my use of birth control was haphazard, but I never once missed a period. When my wife and I wanted a child and I tried to get pregnant—with the help of a friend who shyly handed over a specimen cup of his sperm twice a month—my uterus balked. After a year of DIY monthly inseminations at home, followed by another year of fertility treatments, culminating in a failed in vitro fertilization, my wife and I decided to apply to adopt a child through the child welfare system.

Six months later, our social worker called to tell us that a one-year-old boy would be placed with us. We became parents so quickly we could barely prepare. Friends threw us an impromptu shower and we cobbled together the basics: stroller, crib, car seat, diaper pail. Our son arrived skinny and sturdy, with two teeth, a beautiful name given to him by his birth parents, and, from his foster mother, several boxes of tenderly collected toys, clothes, books, and pictures.

What I didn't anticipate is that even after years of desperately desiring to become a mother, turning into one so quickly threw me completely off balance. As is typical for recently adopted kids, our son regressed. One long daily nap reverted back to two. Favourite foods were spat out. Each night he woke up wailing and one of us would rock with him in the chair my father-in-law gave us, the one that had been used to rock my wife to sleep thirty years before.

My entire life was motherhood. Sleep-deprived, chronically worried, unshowered motherhood. Despite being consumed by parenting in those early days, I also felt like a fraud, as if I had been hired for a job that I was underqualified for, like an entry-level temp suddenly promoted to management.

Maybe most parents feel that they're faking it. In my case, that sense was amplified by the alternately skeptical or overly enthusiastic response nonbiological parents receive from others. I could predict the moment when a parent I was making small talk with in the playground would, after scanning me and son, taking in our different features and skin tones (I'm white and of German and Slovak descent, my son is Anishinaabe), and either ask me where he was from ("Canada," I'd say. "No, *really*, where is he from?" they'd insist) or compliment me for my generosity. ("He is *so* lucky," they'd gush. "Nope. We're the lucky ones," I'd counter with a sigh.) Whether the impulse was condescension or curiosity, it all suggested that I wasn't a "real" mother.

Up until just a couple decades ago, the common practice in adoption was a forced amnesia. Birth records were sealed, past histories erased, and if the adoption was interracial, parents were told to behave as if they were "colour-blind." Along with deepening many adoptees' sense of dislocation, these practices framed adoption as a zero-sum game that cast birth parents as "incapable" and adoptive parents as "saviours." And the narrative of giving an adopted child a "better life," or a "forever family," as our adoption guides put it, too often has required an extinguishing of that child's past, an attempt to render them a blank slate, an empty page.

There isn't a single adoption story, but millions of them. And the complexities of adoption, particularly transracial and international adoption, as well as the histories of Indigenous children being taken from their birth families are too big, too individual, and in many cases too traumatic to be sufficiently covered here. Adoptees and birth parents, survivors of residential schools and child welfare systems have shared their stories of grief, pain, and displacement; no understanding of adoption is complete without those accounts.

These histories shaped how we raised our son. They informed how we carried our obligation to his personal story and to ensuring he was connected to his larger past, to his culture, to his family and kinship network; some of those stories were known to us then and some we learned years later when the three of us eventually met his family. Unlike biological parents, we couldn't locate ourselves in his features or temperament. He didn't have my wife's nose, or my height. But we could recognize and embrace that others had left their traces there: those who shared his broad shoulders, curly hair and big smile, those who passed down his talent for math, his dexterity and tenderness. That's how I learned how to mother my child, the child who is the beloved son of many parents. By realizing that even as I claimed him and loved him fiercely, he was neither my possession nor my creation. He is my child, but he is not mine alone.

In his 2017 book, *The Seeds of Life*, science journalist Edward Dolnick tells the story of a famous sketch by Nicolaas Hartsoeker. The seventeenth-century Dutch mathematician and physicist drew a picture of a spermlike shape and, within the bulbous part, a little person with a huge head, hugging their knees to their chest. As Dolnick writes, it was as if they had "been told to brace for a crash." The rendering was of what Hartsoeker imagined someone might see in the future, when microscopes became more powerful.

As Donick explains, the Western understanding of conception was murky up until the late nineteenth century. Before then, many cultures knew that sexual intercourse between a man and a woman could create a child, but exactly *how* was explained by a mixture of wild guesses, folklore, and religion—that God somehow created children who were then born from women. For centuries, however, the prevailing view was that a full-formed mini-human existed inside sperm—as Hartsoker had depicted. Women merely provided a nourishing place for those humans to develop, like a seed planted in a field.

With women seen as only tangential to the process of creating human life, no wonder early male writers found it easy to compare their creative process to pregnancy and childbirth. The metaphor of creativity-as-birth, after all, is seductive. It transforms the usually unprofitable and often unsuccessful hard graft of writing, and other creative work, into a literal life-giving endeavour.

There are limitations to this metaphor, of course. It separates and flattens both experiences. It expunges the blood, gore, and danger of actual childbirth. It bolsters the myth that the best art is authored by a single (and, let's be honest, *male*) genius while using the imagery of women's labour to describe a creative process they have long been denied equitable access to. (Acknowledging, of course, that not everyone who gives birth is a woman, nor are all women able to give birth.)

The history of women in art is also a history of absence, of a segment of people denied autonomy, means, authority, and access; sidelined as muses rather than makers. The history of women and birth is also a history of violence and danger: rape, enslavement, illegal abortion, forced sterilization, unhygienic maternity wards, unequal access to birth control and menstrual products. It's only in the last century, and only then in certain nations and among certain demographics, that pregnancy and childbirth is no longer full of peril. A World Health Organization survey found that every day in 2017, some 810 women died from preventable causes related to pregnancy and childbirth. In the U.S., Black and Indigenous women continue to be two to three times more likely to die from pregnancy-related causes than white women.

Meanwhile, if birth is depicted in art at all, it's rarely with veracity or depth. Actual labour is viewed with squeamishness and distaste. The 2016 novel *Eleven Hours* takes place entirely during a single labour and delivery in an urban hospital. Its author Pamela Erens wrote that she was drawn to the subject because she felt birth was an epic, transformative event, and she "wanted to show what it felt like to be so very close, simultaneously, to the creation of life and the possibility of death." What more universal, more awe-striking experience could there be, after all? And yet, Erens wrote, one publisher turned down the book on the grounds that a story of a childbirth might be "too specific" and not relatable enough.

What does the enduring metaphor of creativity-as-birth mean for us who don't want to or can't give birth? What does it mean for mothers to have our books thought of as our "babies" and our babies likened to our professional creative work? How does imagining our work as a life-and-death extension of our flesh set the stakes for our work's failure or success?

For me, feeling fraudulent as a mother ran parallel with my feelings of fraud as a writer. Faced with a room of other mothers or writers, I imagine everyone wonders what I'm doing there. Among a certain group of people this holds an element of reality: We have turned both parenting and creative work into a competitive sport, as measures of our worth, as extensions and projections of the self. And when one does both, there are so few positive models, that the sense of not belonging—of not being authentic—is compounded.

For so long, motherhood has been, or been seen as, an impediment to creative work, while the creativity mothers have brought to day-to-day work has been dismissed or overlooked. Motherhood has meant being not being taken seriously as an artist. Outside of being shut out of formally recognized creative work, think, too, of all of the common artistry of generations of mothers never rightfully acknowledged as such: cooking, sewing, beadwork, gardening, hair braiding, lullaby singing. Or, conversely, being an artist has meant not being seen as capable of nurturing others. Consider the trope of the mother-artist as a thwarted, depressed, raging and neglectful shrew. The one who resents her children, who finds domesticity unbearable and stifling. Neither of these options—martyr or monster—is appealing. This dilemma is, I think, what Friedman meant in her distinction of men's *production* and women's *reproduction*. You can't be the subject if you're the metaphor. The biological metaphor of art-as-birth is a trap.

There are other lives, of course, and other narratives. Toni Morrison, single mother of two boys, snuck in 4:00 a.m. writing sessions to produce *The Bluest Eye*, a debut novel published when she was just shy of forty. Reflecting on her creative life as a parent, she wrote:

> [Motherhood] was the most liberating thing that ever happened to me. Liberating because the demands that children make are not the demands of a normal "other." The children's demands on me were things that nobody ever asked me to do. To be a good manager. To have a sense of humor. To deliver something that somebody could use.... The person that was in me that I liked best was the one my children seemed to want.

As Morrison reframed motherhood as joy and liberation, perhaps we might also reframe creativity without the dichotomy or essentializing. We might recognize that childrearing and creativity can be—must be, for some—collaborative efforts. We might understand that there are multiple paths to nurturing and parenting beyond the heterosexual and biological, just as creativity finds myriad forms of expression. We might expand our image of emerging artists to include those who emerge in middle age or later, a time that is often most free and fruitful for those who have children. We might free ourselves of the impulse to sever our creative identities from our maternal identities; and, as well, to subdue our impulse to downplay our creative production by likening it to the more femininely acceptable act of reproduction.

Having a child made writing impossible at times: the demands on my time, energy, and focus emptied me. But motherhood also made writing more possible, too. It's not lost on me that my book—an exploration of modern boyhood and codes of masculinity—wouldn't have existed if I hadn't had my son, and if I hadn't followed the particular path that this particular child, and our particular family led me down. But beyond that, I can't for a moment imagine that any of my work is forged in isolation.

Like my child, my work is the product of many. It's mine but not mine alone.

TWO

BODY

Handicap

LORRI NEILSEN GLENN

Forty-two weeks. At the last checkup, the doctor had measured my belly and muttered something about a small baby. She was new to the clinic, young, but seemed to know what she was doing. "You'll be fine," she said, and I drove the hour back to our house overlooking Hubbards Cove. *But I'm at forty-two weeks, I thought.* That night I felt movement briefly, but it stopped. My husband was out of the province and I debated the wisdom of driving back into the city on dark, snow-covered roads. Who'd watch our seven-year-old?

A golfing handicap is meant to equalize competition among players; the lower the handicap the better the golfer. The few times I have golfed, I've refused to keep score, a decision that annoys others. As a result, I will never have a handicap, nor will I be eligible for one. Anyway, competition ruins a lot of things.

Handicapped parking. This is one of the few remaining uses of a word defined as "a circumstance that makes progress or success difficult." "Handicapped" is now an outdated and offensive term for people with mental, physical, and other disabilities. We have come a long way from the terms "retarded" and "crippled," "spaz," and "feeble-minded." "Special needs" is used so often it has become somewhat of a joke—a phrase that abled people use to mock others. We're encouraged to use "person first" terms: a person with special needs, a person with a disability, yet some prefer instead to refer to themselves as disabled: a disabled writer, a disabled activist.

But however we phrase it, I'm reminded that my disabled son AJ lives in a culture that disables him. He is who he is, but the world insists on measuring ability, quality, and performance.

You are a C-minus person, you are an A person. Competition ruins a lot of things.

Freeze frame: a feeling of urgency, my doctor's averted eyes, the intent focus of the anesthesiologist. I am in the OR, *a barrier—a sheet?—at chest level. Swishing movements, faces in masks, instruments clinking. My husband's breath over my shoulder. I am disembodied, a slab of meat laid out on a table, waiting for the knife.*

Quiet. Rustling fabric. No one speaks. I am waiting for a cry.

There is no cry.

When we downsized to a house in an older neighbourhood last year, I threw out the neon orange traffic cone, an early tactic to try to steal writing time.

Even now, if I leave my room to refill my coffee, my husband might not read the distance in my eyes. "Should I pick up more eggs while I'm out?"

When the spell is broken and my brain turns to the Household Management channel, it can take an hour to be immersed again in my writing. Decades ago, I was relieved to discover research by Mihalyi Csikszentmihalyi; he described the meditative, engaged state of immersion as *flow state*. Flow state grounds and soothes me;

it opens time and lifts me from the quotidian world. Several days away from that immersive state, I am peevish and sour. In my early years, drawing and painting took me there; now it's writing.

When AJ was young, I bought a neon plastic traffic cone at a dollar store. I was desperate for focused writing time.

"When you see the orange cone in front of the door," I said to my family. "That means I'm busy writing. Please do *not* interrupt me unless your hair is on fire or you've cut off your arm."

I faced a tableau of shifty eyes and blank faces. Everyone nodded slightly.

AJ opened his mouth to speak.

"I mean it," I said.

The following afternoon, after a quiet hour or so, I realized the cone trick might be working. But when I lifted my fingers from the keyboard, I could hear breathing. Then, a gentle tap on the door. I ignored it and returned to the poem I was struggling with.

Another tap, this time more insistent.

The door opened a crack. "Um, Mom?"

I stared at him.

"See? My hair not on fire." AJ pointed to his blond mop and smiled. I sighed, ate my lips, and looked into those steady eyes. Silence hummed between us. I didn't dare speak for fear of losing the words I had been about to type.

"And my arm is good."

I could feel the vapour trail of my idea dissipate in the ether. Gone forever.

"What is it?" I finally asked. His face fell. He could read the frustration in mine.

I smiled. I wanted to ruffle his soft hair then, but I also wanted peace and quiet.

"Um, can I—" His speech was often halting. Finding words took time. "Can I have the last Fruit Roll-Up?"

The cursor blinked, waiting.

A language delay. An impairment. How is it parents who studied linguistics and the psychology of reading and writing would have a child who struggled with both? AJ was labelled IUGR, an acronym for intrauterine growth restriction (at that time, the word used was "retardation," not "restriction." Progress, I suppose). I had eaten well, hadn't smoked or had alcohol, so why did my placenta fail to give him enough oxygen? Friends and medical professionals reminded us that, since AJ was born with this disability, who better to raise him?

My husband and I had sailed through school; my literacy level allowed me to skip a grade. We devoured books. But by the age most children speak, AJ had learned only a few words. We read to him regularly, played tapes of stories to calm him at bedtime and to fill his brain with a sense of narrative in the hopes it would help his writing and reading later on. When he began school in our rural community, we feared for him. Overworked teachers have little time or patience for a child who is different. And classmates can be cruel.

AJ became so frustrated with his inability to make himself understood, he'd crawl under his desk. It's impossible to calculate the number of hours we spent with teachers and principals. All I remember is feeling gut-sick for the first decade of my son's life. School was torture for us all.

One winter, after a day on the ski hill, I asked him about his friends at school.

"I can't even say it."

"What?"

"You know. *School.*"

The word came out as a watery slush in the back of his throat. To this day, when I hear someone say *dishtracted* or *shtreet*, I wince.

"They laugh at me," he said. I stirred milk on the stove and added cocoa. *And so it begins*, I thought.

"Okay." I set a cup of cocoa down in front of him. "Have a sip and then do this."

I sat down and opened my mouth as wide as I could. "You try it," I said. "Now make your tongue do this."

Front of mouth. Teeth. *Ssss. Ssss.* Then throat. *Sk. Sk. Sky. Sky. Skoo Skoo. School. School.* Then *Ssss. Ssss. St. St. Story.* That night, he fell asleep practicing this newfound skill, eager for Monday morning. I lay awake, wondering why I hadn't done that sooner. Was I in denial, thinking his skills would come by osmosis? Now in grade one, his speech—speed and articulation—was "behind" according to school norms. And he was smart enough to realize it.

At the time, educators were hotly debating how best to teach children to read and write, many arguing for one-size-fits-all solutions. Guide the child gently; they will absorb words on their own. No, don't do that; teach by breaking down words syllable by syllable instead.

While I was having conversations with graduate students about language theories, at home I had to become the student. As a child, I couldn't be pried from books; as a parent, I couldn't understand why reading and writing would make AJ so anxious he'd beg to escape to a video game. Were we, as his parents, causing him stress? Was it the school culture? I had to park my highfalutin ideas about literacy in the abstract and learn to pay closer attention to my son.

Who had the handicap here? As AJ grew, he taught me to assume nothing, to tread lightly, to listen. To wait. What I learned from him spilled over into my work with writers whose fear and insecurity torpedoed their confidence and skill. But where did that fear come from? A judgmental parent? The teacher who read their story aloud as a cautionary tale? As a mother and a teacher, I still had much to learn.

"Can you come to the school and get AJ?" When AJ couldn't make himself understood in his early years at school, he'd collapse on the classroom floor and wail, and I'd have to bring him home. If the teacher called on him during class, if he made a mistake, if there was too much noise and a swirl of activity, AJ shut down. Language, along with all reason, abandoned him. Talking with other parents of young children with disabilities, I realized he was not alone—overstimulation can be toxic to the brain. It wasn't until AJ was almost a teenager that I began to understand. These episodes were *amygdala hijacks*, a term coined by Daniel Goleman in the mid-1990s to describe emotional responses to threats that shut down the rational brain. Now, twenty-five years later, most people know what PTSD is and most understand the often lifelong effects of trauma and stress on the human brain, but when AJ was younger, I had no language for this. As his parents, we felt helpless.

But what caused him to react so strongly to threat? Did it start in my womb with his struggle to enter the world? Had he absorbed my stress? Was his highly attuned sensory system congenital? All of the above? As a child, he was a fragile antenna and we didn't know why.

Even now, as an adult, we see traces of this. Recently, when AJ received an email with COVID-19 test results, his face was ashen. He could barely breathe, let alone speak.

We'll never know the "what" of AJ's condition; as parents, however, we have had to learn to read him as well as he reads us. We pay close attention. The French philosopher Simone Weil claimed, "attention is the rarest and purest form of generosity." It is also, I claim, an act of love.

Freeze frame: AJ at my breast, days old. His wrinkled skin and large watchful eyes. Old eyes, we said. A five-pound sage whose emaciated appearance took people's breath away. My heart cramped in anguish: will he be okay?

When AJ was a few months old, the pediatrician had told me to prepare for the fact AJ may never learn to read or write. I stared at my wide-eyed baby who was staring at the doctor's stethoscope. The doctor added, "He may need to be institutionalized." The man didn't know that within a few years we'd be in awe of AJ's remarkable memory, the internal GPS that amazed us as drivers, his ability to read faces or emotions in a room.

Institutionalized?

Not on my watch, I thought.

A decade flies by. Children on bicycles, on the tire swing, in the basement. Neighbours in the kitchen. Jeffrey has kicked the dog and she isn't moving. Lynne's car has backed down the embankment; the fire truck is on its way. The pump has broken. Allan collapses from a stroke in front of the stove, mumbling incoherently; paramedics and a babysitter are in the driveway. The next semester, and the next and the next and the next. Screams in the emergency room as the doctor resets one child's bone. Another child stands at the top of the stairs in the public washroom hallway, his pants down, shit all over his legs, howling. A school meeting, and another, and another, and tests, and meetings with a specialist, the next class, the next semester, a snow plough, two, three, a tow truck driver, and another, a plate of spaghetti, endless plates of spaghetti, a rabies shot or two, two kittens, then five kittens, a faculty meeting, then another, a broken leg, the wheel of an overturned car in the hands of a newly licensed boy, the boy's drug habit, school meetings, specialists, theft, a house fire, a renovation, the helpful neighbours and the unhelpful neighbours, two parents' heart attacks, a parent's death, a parent in detox, three sad homecomings, a tongue-lashing from a bitter mother-in-law, a boy sent out of the home, the last few days of a dog's life, a late-night call from the police on the other side of the country, dinners, dinners, bottles of beer, school meetings and houseguests, bottles of wine and houseguests. Gifts of time, life, promise. Loss of time, life, promise.

Try to write it. Try to write? *It's enough to breathe.*[1]

When AJ was in his early teens, I was accepted into the five-week-long Writing Studio program at the Banff Centre. I had managed to carve out an hour or two to write during school hours or late at night. I marvelled at the poet Lucille Clifton, a mother of six children who kept lines in her head until she had a moment at night to write them down. I traded sleep for poetry and finally gathered enough poems for a manuscript. When the poetry mentor called me, I broke into tears. The call broke a dam, touched a raw need I hadn't realized was so deep.

AJ and the family began to understand my need for writing (and alone) time, and I began to travel to find escapes wherever I could: a writers' retreat in a prairie abbey, a sabbatical in Australia, a nunnery in New Brunswick, a borrowed cottage. Like all parents, I knew by then AJ's needs would not lessen, only change.

Care for AJ was an interruption, hampering my work, but so was teaching, worries about his older brother, committee meetings, aging parents, and more. Life interrupts writing—and how was I to write unless I lived it? Years of our advocating for him in the school system ensured he had some support. I used my writing skills to apply for grants, for tuition for a special needs school, to propose changes to benefit not only AJ, but all local learning-disabled children. Soon, after family read-aloud nights of entire fantasy series, years of video games, and later, anime series and a smartphone, AJ learned to read adequately. By then the education system had started to accommodate difference, and, with program adjustments, AJ finished a community college diploma in baking when he was twenty-four years old.

Now at home, AJ shares all cooking and cleaning duties. He's had a series of jobs and romantic relationships, regularly sees friends in the disabled community, and signs up often for programs to improve his work skills. Our ease together as three adults makes me question the (largely) English-speaking world's belief in separate residences for each generation. We plan to build a self-contained unit for AJ's privacy and increased independence. AJ needs a regular support worker to help him stay focused and meet the daily demands of adulthood. For the time being, those support workers are his parents.

AJ has developed strategies to cope with a busy world. He arrives at work an hour early, buys birthday cards and gifts weeks in advance, never forgets a task and the exact time of any event. Speech remains difficult for AJ, however, and learning new tasks can take time.

He works too slowly for some, but he works steadily and accurately. Sometimes his anxiety shuts him down, but usually he asks for help: what to say to rebuff Rogers' sales pitches? How to ask for a replacement or a credit for an item? How to break up with someone in a kind way? The other day a callback from a store manager who had unearthed AJ's resumé panicked him. He already had a job; should he do both?

Anything portending danger can still cause distress. When COVID-19 first peaked, he had nightmares for weeks. Under stress, he has overreacted, especially on social media, and made unwise and costly decisions. Yet I smile as I write this, because these responses to stress are clearly what some would call "normal."

His kindness and gentle nature remain a balm. I live for his wit. The other day I asked if his five o'clock shadow felt itchy under his mask.

"Your beard will grow like mushrooms."

"Yeah, I'm a real *fun guy*," he shot back.

Quick with puns and zingers, AJ is a reminder that so many who are "disabled" have gifts that belie their diagnosis. I want to remind the pediatrician of his comment thirty years ago, and caution him about putting too much stock in medical statistics. While he had warned me then AJ might have to be institutionalized, I'd remind him that AJ has spent years in schools, workplaces and navigating the health care system, all institutions that perpetuate attitudes and practices that can further disable a special needs child.

Freeze frame: AJ's photo in a newspaper feature along with his fellow graduates from the community college, his gentle eyes lit, face glowing.

AJ's monosyllabic responses to questions have become legendary in the family.

"How was work?"

"Good."

"What did you do?"

"Some stock."

"What kind?"

"Crackers."

"That's it?"

"Shelving."

"And . . . and—?"

"LOL."

My husband and I continue to unspool the kite string, watch AJ as he learns to navigate the sky on his own. Even if I am writing, I take his calls and answer his texts. He calls to share a news story, an event at work, a storm warning. Despite his economical speech, he wants connection. Don't we all?

Raising AJ has exposed my own handicaps, taught me patience, and sharpened my awareness of human behaviour. AJ has been the best education I was ever given. Writing is my lifeline to make sense of the world, but it isn't my entire life.

The light in the room tells me it's morning and I could fall back into the dream to find out what happens, but I hear a sound, feel a presence.

"Mom?" Now I'm awake, a bit disoriented. Was that a knock?

AJ is standing beside the bed, a small smile curling his mouth. He's holding a tray with a boiled egg in a paper-towel-lined cup, two pieces of buttered toast, and coffee with cream.

My first thought: *Damn, I'd planned to make coffee and write in bed this morning.* My second and third: *I can't eat this much food this early and cream interferes with my thyroid meds.* Then: *For god's sake, woman, what's the matter with you?*

I sit up quickly and smile at him. "Wow!" I say. "Thank you. You've been busy. And it's only 7:30!"

"Yeah, I was up anyway I thought you might like breakfast." His smile is broader now. "Enjoy!" he raises his arm in salute as he heads down the stairs.

I sip the coffee slowly and take a bite of toast while it's warm.

Some things are more important than others.

AUTHOR NOTE

AJ has granted the author approval to write this essay about how raising him has affected the author's life.

—LNG, April 22, 2021

On Strangeness, Swimming, My Mother, and Me

ERIN WUNKER

> *I believe that always, or almost always, in all childhoods and in all the lives that follow them, the mother represents madness. Our mothers always remain the strangest, craziest people we've ever met.*
>
> —*Marguerite Duras*

Summers beside a lake named for its shape; Gull Foot, shortened in the mid-twentieth century to Gull. When I think of it now, I am reminded of the layers of that word. Shore bird, yes, and also *one who is easy to fool*. What does that mean, *to be easy to fool*? For a long while I fought against the hot vulnerability of gullibility, but perhaps I had the focus wrong. Perhaps sometimes gullibility is close to belief—in magic, or in God. I picture a fish, open-mouthed and gulping. I picture a gull soaring or bobbing on waves. I picture myself, along the edge of that lake and I imagine I am like Narcissus, falling in.

Perhaps it is worth saying something about this lake, even though it feels like it obscures my mother, madness, swimming, and me. But then, perhaps it is just context. We went there in the summers, and later, my parents moved there for good, but that is not this story. Perhaps it is enough to know, for now, that a fish from that lake drew my father's father's family here when he was still a kid. They had been travelling in a tent caravan in Depression America and met a travelling preacher from Canada. They bonded over a shared love of fishing, and later the preacher sent them a photo of an impossibly huge bass. They pulled up stakes, crossed a border, and took up residence in a dilapidated hunting and fishing lodge. It is called Miners' Bay. You could go there, still. When my parents took it over, their webpage still read "no rowdyism." When asked, I would describe it as *Dirty Dancing* run by Baptists, and that is a bit true. Anyway, that's the lake and the reason my father's father got there with his parents, two older brothers, and their belongings in 1937. God and a fish and men bonding over both. This, though, is a different story. Leave the fish. Look at the lake.

There, in the middle of the lake, sitting just below the surface, is a massive remnant of the lake's own becoming. Gull Rock it's called, and indeed the birds have claimed it as their own. Without their white-and-grey bodies sitting, sunning, and floating nearby, without the whitewash of their shit, the rock would be nearly impossible to see. When, at age ten or so, I was allowed to take the motorboat out alone, I would steer as far away as possible from this rock, as if it could throw itself in front of the hull should my attention waver. Now, three decades later, the boat long gone, returned to my mother's cousin Ralph who looked exactly like his Afghan dog, long and lean and loping, I wonder about wavering attention. To waver means to become unsteady or irresolute. Was my attention always wavering when it came to water? When it came to my mother?

Until a few years ago, there was a pipe that ran from the lake right into the house, and while you weren't meant to drink the water, I always thought about it, especially in the shower. Mouth open, face tilted up, I'd let a few warm mouthfuls swish around. Then, scared, I'd spit them into the tub and watch them drain away. The pipe that brought the water to the cottage, which had been there for much longer than I'd been alive, was darkened by weather and well camouflaged amongst rusty pine needles that layered the ground in its own slippery shag carpet. Once, barefooted, I tripped over it and tore the softest part of my big toe. The nail grew back poorly, and for one summer I would sit for twenty minutes twice a day, foot in warm peroxide, my mother coaxing the infection out. Now that pipe is gone, replaced by a new plumbing system after a century of siphoning soft water from the lake.

Gull Foot Lake is where I learned how to swim. Just around the corner from the pipe there was a small area where the granite formed a shallow basin. *The tub*, my dad called it, and it was, sort of. The water in that basin warmed up more than the lake itself, and I remember being small and in that water with my father, who rarely swam, but when he did always wore a T-shirt. In the mornings when I was a bit older, I would come down to the tub and find freshwater mussel shells scattered across the bottom. Evidence of racoons, which, having grown up in the country, I never came to associate with garbage or aggression. I made a pet of one once and marvelled over its small, wrinkled fingers and toes. It, too, liked the tub.

The rest of the lake remains a mystery to me, despite having known it my entire life. It is unfathomable, almost literally in a few spots, and, despite my four decades beside it, it is an enigmatic intimate to me. Even as it is always the place in my mind I go to when reminded to calm down. To ground myself. Strange, to go to water to ground myself.

Though I am prone to it, I dislike hyperbole. Especially now that labelling someone's behaviour as "crazy" has been disavowed in favour of something more nuanced and less repressive. *Say bananas*, we tell our daughter. *Say wild*. Still, when Duras writes "our mothers always remain the strangest, craziest people we've ever met," she has a point. When I think of myself as a mother, it is a bit true. When I think of my own mother, it is a bit true. Possibly very true. She is the strangest person I have ever met. But what does that mean? And what is strange and crazy at a point in history where our relationships to time, space, and place are described with words like *bubble*, *quarantine*, *distance*? At a time when isolation is a virtue?

Regardless, this looping relationship between strangeness, my mother, my writing, and now, my own child, flow together in my mind. Glacial. Aquatic. Wild. Dangerous. I circle these states—mother, maker, monster, me—stalking the edges of consciousness, teeth bared against the dark.

What does creativity look like when your time is not your own? I ask this of a writer friend while the two of us are walking to get our children. What does "making" look like if what you make is dinner and neat piles of folded laundry? What does creativity look like but the development of a complex choreography of time management? Does that count? Will the Canada Council accept documentation of time playing hide-and-seek or managing emotions as evidence of artistic promise? We make fun of ourselves, my friend and I, and then we fall into a silence that, even though familiar, is unnerving.

"There were two otherworlds that saved my life. Swimming and art," wrote one of the many gendered mothers of my literary heart.[2] But I've not written much since our daughter was born. She's five now. Five fingers on a small hand. Five knocks on the door of my heart.

Who am I now?

And what am I becoming?

For all the criticism, there is some of Sigmund Freud's work I still find compelling. His description of uncanniness, for example. And if you take the time to read the essays, there is something wonderfully *unsure* about the writing. After all, this new field of psychoanalysis was an accidental occupation for Freud, and he made many mistakes while conceptualizing and articulating it. As he made these mistakes, Freud recorded them and then published them. This strikes me as remarkable, even after I came across Anne Carson's poem about error.[3] The poem, "Essay on What I Think About Most," begins this way:

> Error.
> And its emotions.
> On the brink of error is a condition of fear
> In the midst of error is a state of folly and defeat.
> Realizing you made an error brings some shame and remorse
> Or does it?

Carson is always a bit tricky, and here she's really on fire. But she's right, I think: error has emotions. When you are about to make a mistake, there is a pricking up of the senses. Georges Bataille called this "horripilation,"[4] literally the hair standing up in terror, but I think of it now as the animal part of me on its hind legs, holding itself as still as possible, and sniffing the air for a sign. And then, just as I'm about to fall into the hole of folly and defeat—of gullibility or worse—Carson pulls the leash. Tug. And I'm back, reminded that error has lessons, and looking always deserves a second glance. In any case, Freud's publication of his own error thrills me for the space it opens.

In "The Uncanny," Freud tries to unknit the question of provocation. Specifically, he's interested in the provocation of feeling that is contradictory to its core: why do we feel both unnerved and familiar toward some things? Never mind for the moment that Freud uses as his example the story of "Der Sandman" by E.T.A. Hoffmann, which, in its panoply of weird characters, settles on the automaton as the central example of uncanniness. Instead, consider this: "[T]he 'uncanny' is that class of the terrifying which leads back to something long known to us, once very familiar."[5]

For two decades, my own mother did something strange. Strange—and thrilling. Strange, thrilling, and then, as time throttled on its own way, predicable. As soon as the lake was warm enough for swimming, my mother would get up early and go. But *early* doesn't quite capture it. She woke at 4:45 a.m., put on her bathing suit and goggles, and walked down over unlit granite to the lake. For years, before my father put in a dock recycled from a great-aunt and -uncle's Airstream trailer porch, she climbed over rocks slick with algae. The water is about waist-deep when you step into it, and from there it drops down ten feet or so. And a little farther on, it drops more. Like all the lakes in the area—and there are many—this one is the result of glaciers passing through. It has crevasses and depths that confound the fish finders on boats of mostly American tourists who come for the bass. In daylight, the lake has a mossy green colour. At night, like any lake, it is black, and into this black water my mother slipped and swam. For nearly an hour, in a darkness pitch-thick and viscous, she swam. A bell jar of black, a blanket of black. A galaxy reflected on the surface of the lake, not yet chopped up by boats and skiers. Sometimes, as a younger child, I thought I could hear her from my room—door open for a crack of light, windows open to catch a breeze. Surely I could hear the soft *one, two, three, breathe* of the front crawl? But perhaps I only imagined it, and, if I'm honest, only imagined waking to listen.

Then, after several years of this routine, there was a boat and she ran into it. Or it ran into her. I can't recall, which seems strange, but there it is. She was swimming steadily and quietly from one point to the next and she bumped into a motorboat. She was terrified and so was the driver, whom she knew. He'd been out fishing, and, mercifully, was pulling into the shore slowly. It is hard to imagine, a large outboard motorboat and my aquiline mother grazing one another. The only images I can conjure are equally impossible: porpoises alongside one another; a prop, a limb, a head face down in *one, two, three, breathe* concentration. Somehow, they hit, and my mother still slipped out of the water and onto shore. Shaken, but unharmed in any way that was visible. And then her patterns changed again, settling further into a strangeness that bordered the terrifying and the familiar.

"The last time my mother took me down to the reservoir, I refused to go into it. It was the middle of the night, late September... I watched her from the shore as she did her circuit. From one end to the other, from one end to the other. There was always a circuit to be completed. There was no moon and I could barely make out her body. She stopped in the middle of the black water and called out, 'Time me!'"[6]

There is, in so many books I have read and films I have seen, a moment when a mother enters a body of water. Often, she startles her daughter when she does this. I wonder at this calculus: woman (usually a mother) + significant and relatively sinister body of water = what? A wavering? A wave? For the women always wave. I thought this most recently while watching the television show *The Queen's Gambit*, where, in flashback, we see Beth start to form a shape of her own bright self while watching her terrifying and brilliant mother surface in the middle of the lake.

Surface, smile, wave.[7]

Shortly after our daughter was born, I received a message from a person I'd never met. She was to be my editor, and I owed her. Of course, she didn't put it like that, but I did owe her, or rather, the press she was with, so it would have been fair. Shortly before our daughter was born, I'd signed a contract with a small press to write a book of an undetermined length, and, in my mind, on an impossible subject. But I was pregnant and unemployed, and, there's no other way to say it, drowning in the unknown. So I said yes, I could write that thing, and I signed my contract, and I cashed my $400 advance to pay some bills, and I shoved the contract in a drawer.

Was this another form of hubris? Perhaps. When I was up at night nursing this small creature, I thought of two things and they were both debts. I owed money. I owed writing. And I was sure I didn't have the cash for either. *Milk money*, I sometimes thought to myself, and while it didn't really make sense, it pushed back the edges of my fear for a moment. But it always came back: inky, thick, claustrophobic. I worried I was feeding her this fear, my child, but always when she was finished, she would unlatch herself and snuffle contentedly to sleep, unwavering in her calm.

After the boat incident, my mother's movements became more extreme. In addition to the foam boogie board she strapped to her bathing suit, an orange pylon appeared on top of it. And on the pylon, a flashing light meant for cycling after dark. And for a long while, a fluorescent baseball cap, worn backward, which was finally discarded when it faded from eye-searing yellow to white and then to what was once-white. The other thing that changed was the route. No more slow steps over roots and rocks to the water in front of the house. Now, she walked down the driveway onto a secondary road, past the wooden bridge that her father and uncle had nearly burned down setting off fireworks in the late 1950s, and into a farther, smaller, deeper lake. Round Lake. This lake is dark yellow-brown in the daylight. At night it disappears into the shore, the blackness of the water connecting with the blackness of the woods, one unbroken, unfathomable line.

On the far end of the lake near the culvert there is a hand-lettered sign painted on chipboard, affixed to an innertube, that reads NO OUTBOARD MOTORS.

I tried to go with her once. Only once. I realize now that I was in awe of my mother, and this made me competitive. This is not a comfortable realization. I was deep in the throes of teenaged disgust—for myself, for my body, for things that felt beyond me, and for things I couldn't name—and this swimming struck me as pragmatic. Something to get out of the way and brag about later. So up I got, and out the door I went carrying my own boogie board and towel. The walk was cool and quiet. The stars were ostentatious. Sleep seeped from my body with each step. My mother brought a flashlight, which was for my benefit.[8] The flashlight, steady in my mother's hand, a beacon of ordinariness. As if its beam of light were saying *see? Just grass. Just trees. Just us walking down a dark road, together.* I said nothing but was grateful.

As it turns out, I could not make myself get into the water. Despite my stubbornness, I could not. There was something about the bottomlessness of it, how everything that touched the water lost its edge. The small, feral part of me bent on self-preservation stopped and held still. It wavered. I couldn't get more than a toe in the water. Water I have swum in every summer since birth. There are photos of me in a pink ruffled bathing suit with the perfect close-capped curls of toddlerhood, smiling in the roped-off swimming area. But there, on the far edge of the lake, well before any part of the sky is thinking about lightening, I cannot. I wave to my mother, who is already several strokes out, and walk home, flashlight in front of me, a little beacon.

One of the places Freud falters as he tries to name that feeling of unfamiliar familiar, of home that is no longer homelike, is around the mother's body. Those feelings one experiences, *this place is familiar to me, I have been here before,*[9] are a waterway memory straight to the mother. The Mother. As if there were a single figure that fits us all the same. What a ridiculous, lazy notion. When I think of The Mother as an idea, I recall the ludicrous proposal by a previous government to build a huge statue of "Mother Canada" facing out to sea, wistfully willing all of her dead servicepeople home. A Cape Bretoner on CBC put a pin in that fantasy when, questioned about his thoughts on the monument, replied *all we see is the arse end of her.* That mother is not my mother. But perhaps that is what happens when some lose their waterways and all of life has clear lines and hard edges and arranges itself just so on the shelf. A particular mother becomes The Mother. An idea. An ideal. A set of expectations to bash heads against.

All the time I was pregnant I swam. I swam, and I avoided deadlines. I swam in a pool at the university. Most days, the lanes were shortened, and I slipped into the water with ease, moving back and forth with a speed that shocked the older swimmers there on lunch break.

Not because I was fast, but because I was pregnant and lap swimming. Back and forth. Back and forth. I stopped for water every fifteen laps and no sooner. I kept this up until almost the day she was born. I kept it up well past the point of being able to do anything after the swim, not even my work. Underwater, time shifted. Underwater, my mind softened its grip on the impossible future I was growing. Underwater, terror couldn't reach me, so I swam. *One, two, three, breathe.*

"Night became my mother's time. She could wander. Night didn't ask anything of her. It did not shame her."[10]

In the end, I wrote for the editor who nudged me out of my own drowning. I wrote for the editor and I wrote for the small girl who made time bend. I wrote in hours snatched from the margins of my life. "The blue hours" Sylvia Plath called them. "That still, blue, almost eternal hour before cockcrow, before the baby's cry, before the glassy music of the milkman, settling his bottles."[11] I wrote then too, in a froth of possibility. There was nothing then between my thinking, my fingers, the keyboard, except the watchful eyes of the dog who died this fall. Writing, I said, brought me back to myself. Now, though, it seems that isn't accurate. I want accuracy. Writing took me out into an inky darkness and left me there to see: sink or swim? I swam, then. But now? Now?

There is a point at which I realize I am no longer wondering "where have I gone," but rather "who am I?" and also "who was I?"

"I am writing—writing with the speed of an animal being chased by a larger animal. The larger animal is time. Here is the artist-mother's bar graph: line one—the multiplying size and need of her expression—held up against line two—the rapid dissolution of time."[12]

Rather than begin with the thing clearly in his sights, Freud starts his essay with troublesome syntax. He piles negative on negative to get to a starting place. It is only rarely, he writes, "that a psychoanalyst feels impelled to investigate the subject of aesthetics even when aesthetics is understood to mean not merely the theory of beauty, but the theory of the qualities of feeling." After cataloguing where a psychoanalyst will first go—"those other planes of mental life"—and then, when all that falters, "it does occasionally happen that he has to interest himself in some particular province of that subject; and then it usually proves to be a rather remote region of it and one that has been neglected." Uncanniness is one of these qualities of feeling. A feeling of falling, of home that is no longer home. Of fear, and of intrigue. What was once most familiar has become strange, the edges that once separated familiar and -un liquefy and lap at the hems of our conscious minds. When we experience the uncanny, we experience that vertiginous feeling of falling into error—or something like it.

This sounds to me less and less like a *remote region of aesthetics* and more like what Hélène Cixous, in a much different text, calls truth or the closest we can come to it.[13]

"I was learning to inhabit water differently."[14]

Freud ends his essay on the uncanny sounding exhausted, which I appreciate. After the avalanche of etymological unpacking, after the analysis of Hoffmann's strange story with its wide-eyed automatons and vision-stealing monsters, after all this Freud lands back in the realm of the aesthetic. He *returns to the scene of writing.*[15] Writing, Freud surmises, is the province of the uncanny. It is perhaps most obvious in stories where the writer wants the reader to feel fear and foreboding. To feel their own little lives watched by some indefinite creature, just off scene. This is the province of the writer—to conjure the strangeness of living and render it palpable, if only for a sentence. But this, against all the rules of strong essay writing, is not where he ends.

Instead, as though he cannot help himself, Freud leaves the reader with this impossible sentence: "Concerning the factors of silence, solitude and darkness, we can only say that there are actually elements in the production of that infantile morbid anxiety from which the majority of human beings have never become quite free."[16]

While his phrasing stinks of the desire to make medical that which is not, still, I like this. I like it, because I recognize it, at least in part. There are echoes here of Duras's claim about mothers and their strangeness. And now, five years into my own mothering, I look into that impossible calculus of silence, solitude, and darkness and see the numbers slipping into place. As I pad down the stairs of my home in the darkness while the sleepers sleep, I feel my childhood stretch both further from me and, strangely, sidle up and slip beneath my arm. Each morning, in the reach for a wakefulness, for the blue hour, I step further into myself. In company, perhaps, with my own strange mother's making.

I experience it—a kind of uncanny mothering, a keeping company, a silent swimming alongside—when I look across the provinces of my own memory and find my mother slipping expertly, strangely, "crazily," perhaps, into fathomless water and gliding away to mark her own time and make her own space. The feeling—call it uncanny, call it age, call it creativity, call it motherwork—is increasingly familiar, for I cannot say what compels me now into dark mornings alone, but there I am. Daily reaching for the blue hour of solitude, the places where the people and the things I love cannot reach me. Well beyond the shore.

The Turning of the Wheel

JÓNÍNA KIRTON

I sit in the board meeting. Before me, the privileged hold court. One of them is my manager, who lives just down the street from me in a fully restored character home. My son and I are basement dwellers, renters of the space no one else wants to live in. I have just left him at Bayview School, where he is enrolled in kindergarten. It was not the usual pleasant walk to school.

There was an incident, not the first, but one of the worst. And now I sit in this board meeting, wearing my one good sweater, a cream-coloured turtleneck. A little too warm for the time of year but it is all I have. I hope no one notices my flushed cheeks. My back feels damp. I pray it is not blood. I excuse myself, and in the washroom mirror I see that it is.

I return to my seat at the board meeting, put my coat on, and pray.

—

My son is in therapy now. At twenty-nine he is filled with questions. I tell him he can ask me anything. He doesn't remember the day I dragged him to school after Dean had thrown me, catching my back on the edge of the coffee table. He doesn't remember the last time we saw Dean or that he had hidden in the bathroom, afraid that Dean was going to kill me and then kill him. He had locked the door, sat on the floor, and waited. He doesn't remember speaking to the police officer who helped us after my son told him what he had seen.

I am afraid his therapist will turn him against me. I am afraid that twenty-four years of sobriety will not be enough.

—

I was going to be a better mother than my mother. I was not going to tolerate the chaos that a man might bring into my home. I was going to raise my son alone. But I got lonely.

—

I did not know that a child tethers you to home and that going to meetings would become impossible. I did not know many things; all I knew was that I wanted to be a mother.

—

I know how it feels to disappear, to be the child in the background of your parents' life. I should have known better.

—

I am afraid his therapist will turn him against me. I am afraid that twenty-four years of sobriety will not be enough.

—

I want to remind him of the good, but that is not what is needed right now. I want to tell him I am sorry, but I have done that. How many times can you say sorry?

—

He hates how many times we moved. All those schools. He says he doesn't have ADHD and I see all those years of effort crumbling. Monthly visits to the child psychiatrist, all the books I read and my interventions with his teachers erased.

—

I am afraid his therapist will turn him against me. I am afraid that twenty-four years of sobriety will not be enough.

—

He has been listening to podcasts. Asks me if I know who Gabor Maté is and I want to tell him how angry Gabor made me when it felt like he blamed mothers for not being the calm, peace-filled bodies their children needed. Instead, I say, yes. Ask, why?

—

I want my son to know why I chose to have him on my own. I mention "toxic masculinity" and I can feel the very thing I always feared is forming in his gut. It is growing tentacles that wander between us. He had no father because I wanted to protect him, and in the end I hurt him because he had no father to turn to. And then when he was three, I was lonely.

—

There was a hole he could not fill. It was a hole that grew large in the night.

—

Can my son understand the fear that grows in a woman's belly? Could he possibly understand how vulnerable I had made myself, a woman alone with a child?

Will he remember how hard I tried? All that I did.

—

I am afraid his therapist will turn him against me. I am afraid that twenty-four years of sobriety will not be enough.

—

He calls me almost every day. He talks and talks. I listen, offer gentle guidance. Pause before I speak. Aware he needs to find his own way; I try not to intervene. He is sorting through the past just as I am writing about the past. I want to make excuses for things he has not even accused me of.

—

I try to write about our first three years. There is a before and after to our shared story. Before Dean and after Dean. Before fibromyalgia and after fibromyalgia. I want to tell him how hard I tried. All that I did. I want to know if this therapist understands the world I was born into, a mixed-race child born to an alcoholic father and compliant mother. I want to know if she knows about racism, sexism, and poverty. Does she know about systemic barriers or will she be like the therapist I had who seemed to blame my parents? I want to know that he and I will be okay.

—

I say to him, "Remember that fight we had? The one just before Jaime died?" It takes him a moment. I say, "It is the only time we ever fought." He has a different idea about it all and something he said years ago surfaces: "Paul asked me how I am getting along with my mother now that I have moved out." I never understood the need for the question and brushed it off as Paul not grasping how close my son and I are. It was a misunderstanding or so I thought.

Perhaps we are not as close as I had thought.

—

My son's therapist has noticed that when he speaks of the things that happened with Dean he is mentally absent. He is disassociated, a state I know well. Gabor Maté has spoken about his mother and the fear she lived with as a Jewish woman during the Holocaust, and how fear is passed from mother to child. I know what my mother passed to me and now I know that I passed it to my son. This is not what I wanted. Does he know how hard I tried? All that I did. I want to make excuses. I want to explain.

—

I go back to that fight. The only one I think we have ever had.

I was asking for help with caring for Jaime, who lay dying in our living room. Jaime was like a brother to my son, a child I never birthed but rather collected in my arms after both of his parents had died. I asked my son, "Why don't you come over more? Why don't you offer us more help? Why aren't you supporting Jaime more? He is your brother. He needs you."

There can be so much unexpressed anger in families. I do my best to speak in a good way, to not let things fester but not everyone is happy with my ways.

—

I am afraid his therapist will turn him against me. I am afraid that twenty-four years of sobriety will not be enough.

—

Jaime was always angry with me. The closer he got to death the angrier he became. When he gets the diagnosis, I want him to come home but we have no home for him to come to. Our one-bedroom apartment will not be enough, but there is another unit coming up in the building.

I call a family meeting and we all sit around Jaime's hospital bed. I try to do it as a circle in hopes that everyone will have a chance to speak. I try to explain that it will be hard for us to support Jaime given the distance between us. I try to say if he lives close we could share meals, watch TV together. I try to explain, once again, the challenges I experience living with fibromyalgia.

—

A year and a half later, Jaime calls. He is alone and afraid. His fiancé has left him. He is hungry but too weak to prepare any food. I say, "I'm coming to get you, my boy." He says, "Okay... but it is just for one night." He will not pack a bag.

It is just for one night.

—

He lies on our couch, thinly folded in half he is barely there. It hurts to look at him. He is weak, too weak to dress himself, but he will not let me help. He sits partially upright, one arm in his sweatshirt and one arm out. Stubborn, he sits half in, half out for an hour as he straddles the change of worlds. One month of this and finally he lets us move a hospital bed into our living room. Care aids scrub the dirt off his body, and there he is again under all that old skin; he is still there, shiny as ever.

The in-home care is cut back. He is dying too slowly for the level of care he is receiving and now it is up to us. Two old farts and a dying boy in their living room. I try to explain how fibromyalgia makes it hard. Ask for more help and my husband sitting next to me says, "Oh no, we are fine."

I shrink back into myself. No one in my family has ever listened when I speak of fibromyalgia. Invisible, I fade into the background of their lives.

I think of my mother and all the ways I abandoned her. I think of my mother planning her exit. The way she wrote her obituary and gave directions for us all to follow. As a nurse, she knew. She knew what was coming.

Even when dying, she thought of others. A few months before her death she called me home to ask if I was drinking too much. She wanted to know if I was happy.

—

My son asks me to come for lunch. We sit across from one another and he takes my hand. He has something to tell me. He has lost his licence. Not his wallet, but his right to drive. He wanted to tell me in person. I feel my energy seeping down to the floor, but it does not stop there. It leaks into the earth below the floor until nothing is left. It is good that he has called me here to this meeting. I need to respond but I am empty of good words. All I can think of is everything that alcohol has taken from my family. All I can think of are my dad's DUIs and how my mother had to drive him to work.

Numb for days, I wander the hallways of the past revisiting the time my father and his brother were the subject of an experiment with Antabuse, a drug meant to make it impossible to drink, but my father drank anyway. Made sick by it all, but he could not stop. I remember my Aunt Eileen dying of liver disease. My Uncle Gordie, one woman on each arm, a wife and four children at home as he headed to the bar. How my mother worried when he came to town. Their mother, Grandma Rose, at the kitchen table rolling cigarettes with a twenty-sixer of rye beside her. But it was not just the Métis side of my family. I recall the fist fight after Grandma Jónína's funeral and the way my uncles made my aunties cry. Alcohol always seemed to bring out the toxic need for control in the men. I wanted better for my son. Did I do enough? He is in therapy now, but...

I am afraid his therapist will turn him against me. I am afraid that twenty-four years of sobriety will not be enough.

—

My son calls to say a close friend has broken his back in three places. He says, "I told him that he could talk to me about anything and that I regret not being there for Jaime. I missed my chance with him. I said I will not do that to you. You can count on me." The mother bear in me stands tall. On her hind legs she rocks back and forth, tries to listen to what is not said. A witness to his awakening, I think there is an apology in there. One that hides within the story and the pride that now sits in his chest.

SAMSĀRA

i
mother I have lost my place
it is dark here mother

without you
the earth is damp
made thin by loss
I am cold
in need of shelter

ii
I have a son now mother
he swims within me
I must build a fire
light the way for your return

iii
he cautions me in the kitchen where I am angry
his small finger pointing, he says,
"I used to be your mother"

iv
I hear a cry
he has touched a hot iron
his lips pouting, and he has that
why would that thing want to hurt me look
I scoop him up, rush to the rocking chair
where I cradle him while he cries
that was until he paused to say
"your mother never did this, did she?"
how does he know this?
was he a toddler remembering another life?
I do not know but he was always reminding me
that he is not just a child, that the wheel turns

Dog Rescue Romance Novels and Other Survival Tools

JENNIFER WHITEFORD

Someone is crying. Someone is crying and I'm trying to ignore it. The book in my hands is helping, drawing me into other spaces where no one is crying. If I can focus on the words, I can leave this stressful place; I can be with these characters, walking dogs through the British countryside, consumed by their feelings for one another, stumbling toward a happy ending.

There were very few ways to pass the time in the waiting room at the fertility clinic.

I was there three, sometimes four, times a month. I quickly exhausted their supply of mediocre magazines. Staring into space was difficult. My eyes were always drawn to the inevitable woman crying in one of the corners of the vast room. Sometimes they cried quietly and sometimes they sobbed openly. Sometimes they were alone but often their partners sat beside them, looking miserable and helpless.

Early on I'd made the pledge to only go alone to the clinic for my appointments. There was no reason for my husband to come with me; never any big news or significant procedures. Just month after month of ultrasounds, checking my wonky insides, gathering data. Every third time they'd tell me to go home and have sex within the next twenty-four hours. They always laughed when they said it, making it sound fun and jokey. It stopped being funny to me after the first few months.

My husband and I had been trying to have a baby for about a year when I was referred to the clinic. The head doctor was a no-nonsense lady with fancy hair and an eternal full face of impeccable makeup. In one appointment, I shared some of the dumb advice I was getting.

"People keep telling me to buy a white carpet. Tempting fate. They say I'm bound to get pregnant then."

The doctor looked like she was trying hard not to roll her eyes. "It's science. We're working with science."

She lacked both a bedside manner and a sense of humour, and I found that comforting. I'm mushy and emotional, likely to cry if people are too nice to me. Thinking of this harrowing fertility business as science made it easier to bear. Science felt foreign to me, a creative person with an English literature degree. It felt easier to have faith in something that I didn't understand.

It was around that time when I bought my first-ever romance novel. I'd never read a contemporary romance novel before, but this one looked good on the shelf of a bookstore so I bought it. It was about dogs. Or rather, a human woman who moves to the country to take over her late aunt's dog rescue. Before I had children, my husband and I had three dogs. I loved the dogs, but I couldn't see them being enough for me indefinitely. Being married and somewhat settled made me realize how much I wanted to have kids.

I brought the dog rescue romance novel with me to the fertility clinic when it was time for my next appointment. It was perfect. The narrative sucked me in right away and it transported me out of that beige room full of sadness. Who wouldn't rather be walking dogs in England while falling for a handsome country veterinarian? I made a point of bringing the book with me when I went to subsequent appointments. I was expecting it to be just a distraction, but it ended up being something entirely different.

The main character in the book gets pregnant. Accidentally. I *know*. I wanted to heave the book into the trash as soon as I read that. And I would have, too, if the secondary plot of the novel hadn't been about the main character's closest friend who was struggling with infertility. All those feelings I had when I read about the character's easy pregnancy happening out of nowhere were mirrored in the response of her friend. Suddenly I was reading a book about infertility while I sat in a waiting room waiting for someone to fix my own infertility. Instead of being distracted by the book, I felt understood by it. It flipped a switch for me, and I began to see the deep value in romance novels. I knew they were often dismissed as "women's stories." *Since when*, I wondered, blinking back tears as I read moving passages in that bleak waiting room, *was that a bad thing?*

When I finished the dog rescue book, I read that author's other novels. When I finished those, I looked up similar authors and read their books, too. Week after week, ultrasound after ultrasound, fictional happy ending after fictional happy ending.

I hadn't always been an infertile woman obsessed with dogs and babies. When I was in my teens and early twenties, I didn't even know if I wanted kids. I only knew that I wanted to write books. I'd had a lot of teenage-level writing success in high school. My short stories and poems were published in literary journals for teens. I wrote various articles and opinion pieces for the local papers. A play that I wrote won a contest and was performed at Young People's Theatre in Toronto. I was also very interested in punk rock and subculture, which led me to the world of independently published, photocopied 'zines. My best high school friend and I wrote down our outlandish teenage adventures and photocopied them ourselves. Eventually I started writing a more serious personal 'zine, *Matilda*, which I sold at 'zine fairs and handed out at punk shows. When I moved to Ottawa after university, I really had only one goal, which was to write a novel. It took me three years to write a YA novel. Because I'd also been writing for the punk magazine *Razorcake*, the publishers offered to put my book out through their small press.

I thought everything would change for me after my book was published. I thought I had become *a writer.* But the book didn't get much traction. I travelled on a few small tours, got minimal media coverage, and had a handful of negative reviews that were so painful to my unprepared heart, I felt like the wind had been knocked out of me. I started talking about my book like it had been a mistake. I thought if I could just move past that YA novel about punk rock and instead write what I called "a Canada Reads book," *then* I would become a successful writer. I tried to write the kind of serious, literary novel that I thought I should be writing.

I failed again and again.

Everything I started writing bored me, or didn't feel "good enough." I read more and tried harder and failed again. One day it occurred to me that maybe I wasn't meant to be a writer. It was depressing but also freeing. I kept writing short essays and music reviews, but gave up on novels. I went back to school. I got a job working for the government. I adopted dogs, got married, and started going to appointments at the fertility clinic.

I was one of the lucky ones. It took a year of monthly monitoring and a few months of drugs (the not-fun kind) and finally I got pregnant. The pregnancy went well, but the birth was traumatic. I ended up having an emergency C-section when my son's heart stopped beating. I had to be put under general anesthetic and I missed the whole thing. I woke up disoriented and depressed. That feeling stuck around for the first year and a half of his life. I loved him, as much as everyone said I would. I took good care of him, made friends with other moms, went outside, ate good food. But no matter how competent and comfortable I may have looked, I never felt quite right. I was scared all the time that something would go wrong. I never felt like I could let my mind relax, which meant my creativity evaporated.

After several months of feeling perpetual, low-key panic, I was exhausted and appealed to my husband for suggestions. On his advice, I went to see my doctor and started taking antidepressants. That helped a lot, but I still had the feeling that my whole life had shifted on its axis and I didn't think I'd ever feel "normal" again. To distract myself, I spent every free moment reading romance novels set in the English countryside. I wrote nothing. If people asked me what I was reading, I would wave the question away like it wasn't important.

"Just romances, you know, 'chicklit,'" I would answer. Nothing important.

It was easy to forget who I was when I became a mother. Being a mom, especially to very young children, is physically and mentally all-consuming. Postpartum depression and anxiety robbed me of any confidence I had. I exhausted myself, making sure that my family was well cared for. I felt like I was the only person who mattered to my children, and felt invisible to the rest of the world.

One day on a family trip to a farm a relative watched a man we didn't know wrangle his kids in the parking lot.

"Wow, look at him! What a good dad!" she exclaimed.

I had literally just done the same thing. When I pointed that out, she said, "Oh, it's different when it's a man."

I love Nick Hornby's novel *High Fidelity*. It follows every structural beat of a contemporary romance novel. That's because it *is* a contemporary romance novel. Couple breaks up, narrator is emotionally destroyed, and, with the help of various zany friends, grows as a person and wins their true love back. That is a romance novel. But no one calls *High Fidelity* a romance novel. Oh, it's different when it's a man.

The romance novel industry is robust and thriving, but strangely invisible to people who aren't directly involved. It parallels the invisibility I felt as a mother.

There were so many things fighting for my mental focus. Did my son need new shoes? Would I be able to pick him up from daycare tomorrow or should I ask my mother-in-law to do it? Did we have enough bananas? The turmoil was internal and endless and secret. I had no room for creativity, but I felt like I should. Like I was doing something wrong. Like motherhood should be more effortless, more natural.

I don't know why I fell for that scam.

I should have known it wouldn't be easy. I knew that Barbara Kingsolver wrote her first novel sitting in a closet so she didn't wake her sleeping children with her typewriter keys. I'd read Grace Paley's words about how being a mother and writer meant that you were endlessly pulled in different directions. I was well acquainted with the fig-tree metaphor in *The Bell Jar*, where Sylvia Plath's main character imagines a fig tree where each fig represents some possibility for her life. Instead of deciding which fig to pick (Motherhood? Career? Art? Travel? Lovers? Athletics?) she imagines herself starving to death because she cannot choose. "I wanted each and every one of them, but choosing one meant losing all the rest." I definitely wondered if choosing motherhood meant that I had lost my other opportunities, especially my opportunity to write. Early motherhood was so all-consuming and full of turmoil, I didn't think I'd ever find myself again.

But eventually, as my children grew, I started writing more and more. I wasn't writing fiction, even though I love writing fiction. I wrote about my kids. Almost exclusively. My long-time friends at *Razorcake* kindly gave me my own column where I could write about the place where parenthood and punk culture meet. That kept me writing and I will always be grateful for it, but I couldn't get my head around turning that writing into anything larger, no matter how hard I tried. I went back to being convinced that I would never publish another book.

What finally pushed me back into being more productively creative was stand-up comedy. I'd always wanted to try stand-up, but never had the nerve and the confidence. As my kids got older, I was better able to fight the guilt that crept into my heart whenever I left them for an evening. Doing stand-up not only made me write regularly and edit all my words into their most concise, best-paced form, it also forced me out of my home. Leaving home meant stepping out of this world where I often felt like a benign but helpful ghost, attending to everyone else's needs. When I was out doing comedy, I was a human again. Not just someone's mom, but an actual person with opinions and talents and funny things to say.

My son had music classes on Saturday mornings and while he was doing that, I would sit in a nearby coffee shop and work on writing jokes. It was at one of those Saturday writing sessions when I first thought, "I think I might be able to write another novel." Somehow it suddenly seemed possible. All it took was remembering that I was a person.

In the end, it was the stresses of motherhood, not the joys, that led me to finally complete my second novel. In the spring and summer of 2020, bogged down with the responsibilities that came with working full-time while also parenting children in the middle of a global pandemic, I finally wrote. I had limited time and severely depleted energy, so I was forced to think hard about what I wanted to write. I wanted to write something that would bring me joy and keep me going. I wanted to write a romance novel. And I did. It's imperfect, needs heavy editing, and I don't know if it will be published, but it's done.

And even after years of gaining respect and understanding of romance novels, I still caught myself occasionally playing it down. "I wrote a book over the pandemic, but it's just a romance, no big deal."

But it *is* a big deal. Just like so many other things that mothers do. There are so many big deals around us that we turn into small deals. Or that the world around us turns into small deals. I'd like to say I now have confidence in myself both as a mother and a writer, but in a way this part of my life is just beginning. I still can't write a chapter without being interrupted and asked for a snack or a charge cord or a hug. But at least there's somewhere else for my mind to go these days.

Someone is crying. Someone is crying and I'm trying to ignore it. The text on the screen is helping, drawing me into other spaces where no one is crying. If I can just be pulled into the writing for five minutes, even those five minutes will help. Five minutes spent away from the messy reality where there are no happy endings because nothing ever ends. For now, that is enough.

Tantrum Series

TERESA WONG

My son, a few months shy of three years old, comes out of his room in the morning, having slept late. Rubbing his eyes he asks, "Where are the sisters?"

"They left for school before you woke up," I tell him gently, knowing he'll be disappointed. His siblings are the demigods in his pantheon, the heroes of his small life.

"Don't say that," he demands.

"Sorry buddy, but they're not here," I say. "They'll be home really soon, though."

"NO, DON'T SAY THAT!" he screams, a flash of red pajamas running down the hall to search their room.

"But I can't change where they are," I say, knowing it's already too late to reason with him.

Clearly as a funnel cloud touching down on the flat prairie horizon, I can see what is coming next. Toddlers control the weather, and it is time to take cover.

"NO, SAY THEY ARE IN THEIR ROOM!" he cries, flopping onto the carpet in a burst of tears and thrashing.

A mother of three, I have witnessed scenes like this many times over the years and have already tried numerous approaches to calm and soothe my children during their countless tantrums. What I've concluded by this point is that there is nothing I can say or do to resolve things. Part of motherhood is feeling helpless and then sitting with that feeling for... I don't know... ever, I guess? Swept up in his own "big feelings," he is not even totally present. I can only stay with him and make sure he doesn't hurt himself.

But, this time, I do one other thing: I grab my iPhone and surreptitiously take a few photos.

"For reference," I tell myself.

After the tantrum has ended and we've had a pleasant morning playing with Play-Doh, after his sisters come home and everyone works on a Duplo castle, after the merest bit of screen time, and after a whirlwind of dinner and cleanup and baths and bedtime stories, I sit down at the kitchen table and stare at the image of my son in mid-tantrum.

I get out my paints and do a quick watercolour sketch, trying to capture the intensity of his expression, as well as the sweet, plump lines of his cheeks, his hands, his feet.

As I make the portrait, I feel a strong compulsion to go upstairs and lift him out of his crib, to feel the full weight of his little body on mine, but I know better than to obey that urge. You don't survive three kids in five years by waking them up whenever you feel sentimental. You never wake them unless it's absolutely necessary. And even then, you never, ever like doing it.

I look again at the pictures of my son. They are visceral. You can almost feel the energy coming off his twisting body.

He looks fully alive and fully himself.

I posted the finished sketch of my son's tantrum on an Instagram account I'd started earlier that year to try to build an "author platform" (whatever that means). I had recently signed with a literary agent in New York, and she told me that a social media presence might be helpful in making my manuscript more palatable to big publishers. I began posting daily drawings—some funny, some earnest—mostly centred on my family life.

My #tantrumseries grew out of that daily practice because, with a toddler in the house, so many of my days involved tantrums. At the time it seemed to me that motherhood on Instagram was portrayed mainly as art-directed vignettes of cheerful children in curated environments wearing shades of grey, denim, and cream. I wanted to present something more ordinary, more realistic and, I hoped, a faithful record of my own experience as a mother.

The series was also extremely funny to me, especially when I quoted my son for the title of each portrait. "No Daddy, Just Mommy" and "I Don't Want to Because I Don't Want to" have the feel of found poetry, and still make me smile years later.

But as the number of tantrum portraits grew, I began to feel conflicted. Was I harming my current or future relationship with my son by posting these images? Was it at best unfeeling or at worst unethical to use my child's emotional pain for an artistic pursuit? And was a social media post even art? Was it all just for the likes?

Or was I depicting something other mothers needed to see in order to feel a little less alone as they too wrangled their writhing, unrelenting creature-children? Was the #tantrumseries an accurate depiction of life as a mom, and therefore an affirmation of sorts?

In a 2016 *Vela Magazine* article about motherhood and Instagram, author Sarah Menkedick writes about how posting pictures of her daily life was motivated in part by wanting to elevate the quotidian above the epic, and to "lend validity to a life that is often invisible." She goes on to add, "the domestic life of women and children, in spite of its cheery ubiquity in advertising, is largely hidden, belittled, oversimplified, ignored."

It's true. I wanted others to see the storms of emotion that passed through our otherwise nondescript suburban home, to see the big in the small. I also needed it for myself, a reminder to pay attention to life as it unfolded in front of me, whether I liked it or not. As the cliché goes, the days are long, but the years are short, and I knew my son would soon outgrow the tantrums and never really look like that again. His facial features would sharpen and come into clearer focus, his body would lengthen, and the baby would melt away.

I stopped in the end, not because of my own ethical concerns, but because he began to notice whenever I took out my phone to snap a photo of him.

"Don't take my picture!" he would demand. So I didn't. And I wasn't a good enough artist to draw without a reference.

Now, at age six, he'll sometimes scroll through my Instagram posts to look for images of himself. He seems unbothered by my paintings of his tantrums, probably because those moments don't register as memorable in his young life.

In fact, whenever he finds one, he smiles and says proudly, "That's me!"

When I look at the portraits now, I see that there may be more to them than I'd originally thought.

David Hockney's 2016 exhibition *82 Portraits and 1 Still-life* was born in a time of crisis for the artist, a time when he found himself unable to paint or draw for several months. He fought his way out of the darkness by returning to portraiture, embarking on a grand project to paint his wide circle of friends and acquaintances.

I'm no Hockney, but I now realize that I, too, was going through a crisis of sorts when I started #tantrumseries. My manuscript had gone out to a large number of publishers in the months previous, and they had all rejected it, saying the story was good, but they just couldn't see it "breaking out" in the market because of its topic: post-partum depression. One editor wrote that he didn't think mothers who had been through PPD would ever want to relive it by reading about it.

Not everyone, it turns out, feels the need to lend validity to a life that is invisible.

The week before I painted the first tantrum portrait, my agent dropped me, telling me over email that there wasn't anything else she could do for my book. In that moment, it felt like all my hard work had been for nothing, and my hopes for publication were crushed.

These days, I look at the twenty paintings I made of my little boy, lying on the floor, crying with abandon, and think about the woman who was standing over him each time, feet just out of the frame. I

remember her and how hopeless she felt about her creative life, how much she wanted to lie down next to her son and howl too at the injustice of it all.

Most of the time I don't know what I am making while I'm making it. I work by instinct and impulse, putting down line after line until something comes to life on the page. Until it gathers a certain mass, the work is formless and fragile, extremely sensitive to light and quick to dissolve. The key is to hold open a space long enough for it to grow and become a real thing.

I believe that mothers in particular have trouble doing this because we have neither space nor time. Instead, we have a giant load of guilt, which manifests itself in many ways, but almost always comes down to a single question: "Will doing this creative work that feeds my soul damage my child somehow?"

The thing is, I'm pretty sure I know the answer now, and I think you do, too.

Keep going. Don't worry about whether it's good or right or taking too much time. Don't worry about how your work will be received.

My book was eventually published, and the tantrums are mostly in the past. But the creative impulse remains, disruptive and uncontrollable as ever. My only job is to stay with it, and to let it become fully alive and fully itself—just like the child in my care.

THREE

SPACE

Making Space

NIKKYA HARGROVE

After a submitted application, after the interviews were finished, the email came in. A confirmation of what my intuition had already told me; I'd been accepted to a one-week writing residency in Brewster, New York. Not only for me, but also for my twin daughters, who had just turned four years old.

The SPACE Family Residency at Ryder Farm was an opportunity suggested by my sister-in-law, a playwright who sat on the board, who told me the applications were open and that I should apply. I'd never applied to anything like SPACE before and was nervous from the very start, opening my laptop, Googling and then reading about the program. The residency offered the opportunity to fulfill a lifelong dream of mine; to be a good mom and to do so while doing what I love—writing.

At the time, I was also in the throes of working with my literary agent to find a publisher for my memoir, *Mama: A Black, Queer Woman's Journey to Motherhood*, fielding rejections and then picking myself up again. This acceptance letter was a welcome relief, and a reminder that I was on the right path—seeking out opportunities not only to write, but to also mother my kids and feed my soul.

I'd spent my career working in the nonprofit sector, helping others get to a better place in their lives, helping them over the hurdles they could not jump over alone. Writing was what did that for me; it pushed me through challenges I faced in my life, gave me the ability to "write it out," and in turn work toward letting go of whatever worried me, haunted me, troubled me.

Writing was how I was able to deal with my mother—her multiple incarcerations, her absence from my life, her addictions to money and men. I have the journals to prove that writing got me through, and though they are weathered, I still carry them with me.

I carry them like I carry the scars I wear on my belly, the stripes from my pregnancy with my twin daughters.

Life has a funny way of taking us exactly where we need to go and delivering us right on time. That's how it happened for me; I was in the right spot, at the right moment, ready with open arms and waiting for love when I met my wife, Dinushka.

In our very first email exchange, I told her I wanted to become a mother again. We began talking online in the early weeks of August, the summer just after my own mother died at the age of forty-two. I'd tried online dating once before, but there was something different about the feeling in my stomach this time, the butterflies that found their way into my belly every time I opened an email from her.

A month after our first correspondence, we decided to meet in person, and from that day forward we've been inseparable. My son was eight months old then, and Dinushka thought time would change my heart, my call to become a mother again, but it never did. And from the morning sickness, to the stretching of muscles I never knew I had, to my scheduled C-section, the birth of our daughters reignited the spark of my other calling—to be a writer.

I wanted to write full-time, to spend my days hopping from café to café, filling up pages in my journal. I daydreamed about finishing a book a year, being a published author, one who would be able to feed her family off of those daydreams. But I never really thought my dreams would come true, and in many ways, they've not. I still feel as though I am living the dream, though—I get to write every single day, and get paid for it.

There are days I am too tired from hopping from my bed to one of my daughter's because she is too afraid to sleep alone. There are days I want to get down on the floor and play with Barbies, but am called to the page. The struggle to show up for my kids and for my work demands a Wonder Woman kind of strength, the kind that drags me out of the bed at 5:00 a.m.

Today, when I tell my kids I need to write, they understand, even if they don't like it.

Like my kids, the blank page accepts me as I am. All I have to do is keep showing up. To make time to get the words down—some of which I'll keep and some of which I'll lose—takes effort. What I am grateful for is that I have the ability to do what I love; mother my kids and show up for my writing.

While my twin daughters learn to swim at the Y, I can write from the small bench that sits steps away from the pool. I can write when my fourteen-year-old son Jonathan is in his forty-five-minute-long piano lesson. I can be there for them, and I can be there for my writing. It is not always easy to do, but for me it isn't a choice between one or the other—I must do both.

Getting to the place where I had the courage to put the whole truth down on the page has taken me twenty years. When I was an undergraduate at upstate New York's Bard College, I clung to a secret that has turned into my memoir—my mother was never there, and instead found a home far away from her responsibility to me. I spent my life hiding the fact that I was the daughter of a woman who chose selling drugs, a woman who chose jail, prison, and a life of crime over raising me. My mother was both physically and emotionally unavailable in ways that I will never repeat with my own kids, not even to write.

In 2005, while I was preparing to graduate from Bard, I was also preparing myself to go pick my mother up from a three-year prison sentence. I told no one where I was headed that cold March day when I took a trip to New York City and my mother was released into my custody. I was only twenty-four years old.

Now, as I write my memoir—a story about how, as a gay, Black woman, I became a mother when I didn't have a very good example of one—I reflect on my relationship with her. The ability to "go there" in my writing, to access parts of myself that I'd long placed under lock and key, weighs on me. It forces me to retreat to the young woman I once was, without my own children, my only job to be my mother's keeper.

I try to write before the sun rises, get the words out before my kids wake up, or work for an hour or two after I put them to bed. At bedtime, I kiss them on their foreheads and tell them I love them. I watch them as they drift off, secure in who I am as their mother. I close the door to their bedroom, their astronomy lights glowing back at me, and I take a deep breath in—and then breathe out the tiredness.

From the moment I pick them up from school, through dinner, and books, and bed, I have parented them, and then I get ready to bring my A-game to my other job as an author.

My writing has evolved over the years, from journal-writing, to dabbling in non-fiction, to freelance work, and now I will be a published author. My creative process has not been a straight path, and neither has my journey to motherhood.

There were years when I put words on paper, never expecting anyone else to read them. There were times when I pined away for that one email telling me my pitch was accepted. I think about all of the rejections I have received over the years, and it stings quite a bit. But writing is like motherhood; when those rejections come, as they are guaranteed to, I pick myself back up again because writing—like my kids—gives me life. It is with me no matter what. It is what keeps me going.

And for me, becoming a mother meant acceptance after years of rejection from my own.

My teenage son has long pegged me as the parent who can't do anything right, the one who nags him and asks him to clean up after himself. I am often the one blamed for all things wrong in his life. I am the reason he cannot wake up on time for school, the reason he can't eat junk food, or ride his bike without a helmet.

"Gosh, you just don't get it" are words I hear from him far too often.

In some ways, my son reminds me of all of the agents and editors over the years who have rejected me. Both feel equally harsh, both forcing me to put in the emotional work needed, asking me not to be paralyzed or knocked down by the words that, in time, will make me a better writer, a better mother, and a stronger person.

If nothing else, my son gives me lots of material to draw from, topics to write about, feelings to tap into. He is a living, breathing reminder that my work as a writer is not something I can do alone. I need him as much as he needs me, even if he doesn't recognize it yet.

When he was a baby, I journaled while he slept, writing down the memories I had of my mother before she died. In the first few years after his birth, I worked to put food on the table, to put myself through a master's program, to provide us both with a roof over our heads, and for a short time did so as a single parent, until I met Dinushka in 2007.

I put my desire to be a writer on hold to give him the opportunities I felt he deserved.

The pandemic arrived just before that summer I was due to attend the SPACE Family Residency. The one-week opportunity would have been a place for me to write during the day while my then four-year-old daughters would have a camp-like experience, supervised by SPACE staff. We would all come together at lunchtime—kids and creators—to build community and break bread together. Instead, the SPACE Family Residency and our place in it was put on hold.

My hope, for that one week, had been to bond with my daughters in a deeper way, to connect with my writing by giving it big chunks of my time and attention, secure in the knowledge that my daughters were safe, happy, and making friends. That they were living the summer dream like any other four-year-old would have if it hadn't been for COVID-19. Living through the pandemic changed our summer plans and required me to pause my writing, pushing my creative self to another time when I was able to think about anything other than keeping my family protected, healthy, and alive.

Over the years I have worried that there was no way I could be both a mother and a writer and do either well. But as far back as my memory goes, I wanted all of it—the morning sickness, the indigestion, those stretch marks across my belly—because the end result, if all went as planned, would be a baby. That's also how I feel about writing; rejection is the morning sickness of the writing process, and each response is one step closer to an acceptance.

With writing, I am accepting my craft as a gift. I am showing up, letting my words spill out onto the blank page. They arrive exactly when they are supposed to. They arrive prepared to help change one person's life—or at least their perspective—giving the reader an opportunity to understand someone like me. But that does not happen without my community of family and friends. My partner is the one who runs through our house with the kids, playing a very good game of hide-and-seek. She is the one who takes them sledding, or on long hikes in the summer to give me time. Then there are our friends who have offered me their empty rooms to write in. My community shows up for me as a village, providing me with child care or a personal editorial team. They allow me the time and space I need to do the best writing I can.

The beauty of writing, the reason I love it, is because it travels life with me, gives me pause, helps me step back from the mess of it all, and puts things into perspective. And while the act of writing is done alone, it cannot be done without help. It is my community that—even on the days I feel rejected—keeps me whole, and supports me to be the best mother and writer I can be.

Death of a Muse

S. LESLEY BUXTON

Our house is divided into two apartments. In the summer we rent out the upstairs apartment to vacationers and live downstairs, and in the winter we move upstairs. It's like living two realities.

When we first moved downstairs to the smaller apartment, my husband, Mark, built me a set of shelves that remind me of an old haberdashery cupboard. All different sizes, they are now crammed with my favourite things: mason jars filled with buttons, tins of ribbons and threads, baskets of yarns and fabrics. Often, when I'm supposed to be writing, I distract myself by taking down one of the many containers and reorganizing it.

Alongside these things are books, photos, and strange keepsakes, like a toy double-decker bus with a broken wheel, and a vintage tape measure in the shape of a cat. There's a small gold-plated Ganesh that I sometimes like to cradle in my hand for comfort. It used to belong to my daughter, Indy. An atheist friend of mine gave it to her. For years, the God known as the remover of obstacles sat on a little ledge over her bed. Now it sits on a shelf above her urn. Since her death it has moved many times.

Indy died eight years ago when she was sixteen from a rare neurological condition that began when she was ten. In six years, she went from being the kid who climbed the highest on the rope at gymnastics to having constant seizures that made it impossible for her to walk or use her hands. She was my only child.

When people find out my only child died, they often ask why I had only had one. They used to ask me this question when Indy was a toddler as well. Back then, I ignored it. I just figured they envied our closeness and freedom. When Indy first died, this question offended me. Now it makes me laugh. What do they mean when they ask this? Are they saying I should have expected to be bereaved, and prepared with an extra child? Or that if I'd had another child it wouldn't matter? I don't understand; I have two arms, if I lost one of them, I'd still want the other back.

I only ever wanted one child. Early on in my writing practice I remember reading an Alice Walker quote that said something like a writer should only have one child because she needs her other hand to carry her typewriter. I looked for this quote while I was writing this but couldn't find it. I did find this about writers written by Walker: "They should have children—assuming this is of interest to them—but only one."

Why? "Because with one you can move," she said.

Did my child make me a writer or was I a writer before that? This is a question that I constantly circle back to.

Before Indy's death, I never considered how entangled those two selves were: the mother and the writer. Now I find myself thinking about it often. Ours was a relationship bound by creativity. Indy sang and danced for me. I told her stories as we walked to the park or waited for the bus.

I have always loved stories. If I close my eyes, I can still conjure up the memory of my mother reciting Robbie Burns' "Where Helen Lies" to me in her soft Geordie accent. I was only about five years old, but I was seized by the drama. I used to act out the tale and pretend to be Helen's lover weeping on her grave.

The Lady of Shalott, Rapunzel, Snow White, Persephone—looking back, I realize all the stories of my childhood featured teenage girls in torment.

Back on a humid Sunday evening in early April 1997, I remember scurrying around my bedroom in my underwear, searching for something to wear. I was eight months pregnant and two hundred pounds, so heavy my thighs chafed when I walked. Everything I owned was too small. I was going to my first creative writing class in a long time, and I wanted to look good. Ever since I'd found out my new neighbour, a writer, was giving workshops, I'd had a soft fluttering in my belly that made me feel like I'd swallowed a butterfly. The last time I had this feeling was after my first date with my husband.

In those days I carried a small black notebook wherever I went, thick with unfinished stories and poems. Often I'd write the first line of a story over and over, gradually adding lines before I got stuck and gave up. I was like the kid who climbs up on the diving board for the first time, only to become frozen with indecision—unable to jump or turn around and climb down the stairs. My problem was I didn't have any discipline or faith in myself. I thought I had endless time to fix that.

When faced with motherhood I was starting to realize I didn't.

As a teenager in the 1980s, some of my mother's friends scared me. They had a way of looking at you that made you feel as if they could predict your destiny. One woman in particular used to stare at me as if I were a sacrificial sheep, and she a Delphic oracle.

Young as I was, I understood the problem was envy. Like me she was artistic, but unlike me she'd never had the opportunity to chase her dreams. I never wanted to look at my child that way. I wanted my child to be proud of me.

That night, I lay in bed repeating a mantra that I have repeated over and over ever since.

I will not stop writing, I will not stop writing, I will not stop writing.

My current writing desk sits facing Indy's urn. My view is obscured by my computer screen, though I'm always aware it's there. Sometimes I wonder if someone broke into our apartment, would they know what the urn was? At first glance it looks like it might be an expensive antique Chinese vase.

To those who have not a lost a child, my desk facing the urn might seem morbid. I imagine there was a time when I might have agreed. I don't see it that way now. I like being close to her.

Lately I've been leaving things around Indy's urn—the tiara she wore on her sixteenth birthday, a photo of her best friend Aly holding her university diploma, a little silver heart-shaped box she gave me. These things remind me of the small shrine that sits in front of the bar at my favourite Vietnamese restaurant. As a toddler, Indy was mesmerized by it. The glow of the yellow lights shining against the small red lacquer altar, the sticks of incense, the plates of fruit, and the small china bowls that looked like toy teacups. Sometimes I imagine I will begin to make offerings to Indy, little plates of gummy bears, fuzzy peach sours, pictures of boy bands, her favourite manga, and cans of ice tea.

In my head I'm constantly chatting to her. It strikes me that talking to Indy isn't that different from writing a story. Both are an act of faith that someone is listening.

Indy was my muse. I needed to serve someone I loved more than myself in order to gain the discipline I lacked. During our first months together, while she napped, I fought tiredness to write. By the time she was a toddler, I'd sometimes let her watch TVOKids all morning so I could finish a story.

Like all muses, Indy could be unpredictable. She'd refuse to nap or wake up unexpectedly just as I was getting somewhere in my work. By the time she was in kindergarten she would sit at my desk and play with my old computer, pretending she was a writer, too.

There were days I envied my writer friends without children and their freedom. My progress was slow. When Indy was nine, I went on a writing retreat for two weeks. She phoned every night to tell me she missed me. It took me days to shake the feeling I was a bad mother—a feeling that still haunts me.

Once when she was thirteen, Indy saw me writing and, in one of those dismissive tones that teenage girls are expert at, asked, "How can you be a writer? I hate writing. It's so boring." She didn't say it to hurt my feelings, but it still did. I knew it shouldn't. I tried to shake it off, but I just couldn't. It's a child's job to disengage and become independent, and part of that process is rejecting their mother. I told myself I should be proud that she was confident enough to tell me her thoughts. Even so, I cradled my wound.

When it became clear Indy was probably not going to get better, I was working on a short story collection entitled *Walleyed* that I'd been writing on and off for ten years. She was spending more and more time sleeping, and her neurologist was running out of drugs and suggestions. The stories were the ones I'd started writing all those years ago when my Indy was napping. Many of them had been published in magazines I admired, and I was proud of my blossoming publishing history. I'd sent the collection to an author who helped emerging writers and she'd been encouraging. Going through her notes, I knew I was close—I was at that delicious point where I could finally see the ending.

This was where I stopped. I told myself I would just take a break. I would return to it once Indy was stable. She was dying, though I couldn't admit it.

During the day, I sat at the end of Indy's bed, sewing or knitting while she slept. Unless I was holding my daughter, my hands were never still. In the evenings, I read blogs on grief and loss. I was searching for a manual on what to expect so I could prepare myself.

I didn't abandon writing completely. I continued working on the blog I created about mothering a child with a rare illness, hoping some doctor would read it and suddenly appear with a magical cure. Of course, that never happened. People did listen, though. There were letters from all over the world—mothers with children with rare illnesses, bereaved parents, people writing with prayers, all writing to assure me I was not alone. Since then, I have written only creative non-fiction, primarily about grief. My collection of short stories has remained untouched. I dream of returning to it, but I doubt I will. My stories seem trivial compared to the reality of my life. These days I even struggle to read literary fiction, which used to be all I read. I can't seem to become emotionally involved in a story unless it's true. I hate this. I miss the fabulous feeling of sinking into a great piece of fiction. Still, I continue to buy novels, determined this will change. There are piles throughout the apartment like stone cairns, mapping my boundaries.

As a bereaved mother, I endure by avoiding the trappings of motherhood and the intrusions of memory, but as a creative non-fiction writer it's my job to observe and recall. The push and pull of this dichotomy is not an easy state in which to survive. I'm both the bereaved mother, who frequently hides herself and her muse in the company of other mothers, and the writer of creative non-fiction, who is driven by the ghost of her muse to revisit her most painful memories.

Over the years I have written on many different desks. My favourite was a wide wooden 1930s desk that I bought at a government auction. It reminded me of something that might have belonged to Virginia Woolf. When I wrote on it, I felt like a character from a Graham Greene novel. I lost it when we moved from Ottawa to an 1880s house in rural Quebec. It was too wide for the narrow staircase.

Now I write on a rickety kitchen table that a friend found at the apartment building he manages. I have to be careful not to type too hard or it shakes. Here, everything is divided into piles of the finished and the unfinished—there are writing pads with lists of ideas for essays that I've abandoned, finished to-do lists lined with black marker, new and used notebooks.

When we still lived in our house in Quebec, where my daughter's presence clung like dust to every belonging and room, I had a dream I've never forgotten. In the dream, Indy is dancing on a small green island floating down a fast-moving river. She wears a long crimson dress with a stiff black taffeta underskirt. Her bodice is embroidered with gold threads that spiral like flames across her chest. She looks as if she belongs in a production of Stravinsky's *Firebird*. Colour sparks from her heels as she paints the air with her pirouettes. I watch her from a battered yellow long-tail boat. My boat is still, but her island is caught in the river's current, and with each step she takes she floats farther and farther away.

If she feels bad that she's floating away from me, she doesn't show it. Her green eyes are bold.

Mark and I now live downstairs in a place that Indy has never visited. On the way upstairs, on the wall, there is a portrait of her, her blue violin, and two ceramic birds that guard it. Other than this, there isn't much here to connect me to my former life. We designed this apartment to look appealing to the discerning Airbnb customer. Personal effects are minimal. When we move upstairs again, I will bring my baggage with me—the photos of my girl, Indy's Ganesh, her shrine, and this old table, so I have something to write on.

From time to time I find myself cataloguing all the things in our new house that Indy never touched. I do this and marvel at how she can be so close and far away at the same time.

"I am mother, wife, Muslim…"

Creativity, Feminism, Motherhood, and Academia

AMBER RIAZ

The day I met Canada's Rockies,
I wrote a million silent verses.
You were a writer, they said.
I used to be, I said.
But when I got married,
my hennaed hands
learned to hold wooden spoons
and forgot the feel of a pen.
My poetry melted
into the curries I served,
and my spirit sang to new tunes.
It used to be, I said,
that my heartstrings
thrummed to words

woven, tapestried.
But now, I said,
I thrive on "I love you" from young lips.
I still write, I said,
But now I write only on my heart.
I find poetry in little smiles,
in belly tickles,
in bedtime chats,
in magic kisses,
in game nights and movie nights.
My poetry melts
into curries and chapatis:
feeding my soul, their bodies.
You are a mother, they said.
I still write, I said.

When I first started working on this essay, I thought to myself, what could be easier than writing an essay on being a Pakistani Canadian mother with a (hidden) creative streak? In my head, I was going to speak from a position of authority. Who better to talk about being a South Asian academic mother with a strong creative streak than little old me? I identify as a "visible minority" on all the relevant government forms, and even place a check mark on the "South Asian" box when it is available. I have completed my PhD (rather impractical, given that it's a liberal arts degree) and did so while maintaining the busy schedules of my young children (who were nine and four years old when I graduated), and my husband (who worked rotating shifts during those years).

In my proposal for this essay, I talked about the multiplicity of my identifications and the complex web of emotions that result from that multiplicity. After numerous false starts in writing it, however, I have been forced to confront my own insecurities first. A nagging voice at the back of my head continuously taunted me:

"Who are you to talk about 'being South Asian'?"

"You didn't even use that label until it became fashionable in academia all those years ago."

"What do you know about mothering? You're still learning!"

I found myself deleting the words I had written.

The tyranny of the blank page—or laptop screen—began to eat away at me and the deadline began to loom large on the horizon. I found myself panicking, knowing in my bones that "I am a writer" rings false. I have long believed that I will become a writer, but I am now in my midforties, with almost-grown children, a career that just doesn't seem to be going anywhere, and a nagging belief that I have nothing of value to say.

The problem of the opening sentence remains: Where does one begin to talk about South Asian Mothering in Canada? How does one begin to express one's creative streak? What even *is* a mother's creativity?

I grew up in Karachi, Pakistan. We were all taught to use the word *subcontinent* to refer to the region south of the Himalayas, and which now includes Pakistan, India, Bangladesh, Nepal, Sri Lanka, Afghanistan, and Bhutan. At that time, I had no idea that a term like South Asia existed. *We were Pakistani—NOT Indian!* We learned very early on to, if not hate, then at least dislike everything Indian.

Of course, the pull of Bollywood could never be denied. Friday afternoons for us meant bundling together into our parents' bedroom (it was the only room with an air conditioner), popping in the latest Bollywood videotape (we never called it VHS), and then listening to our daadi (paternal grandmother) maintain a running commentary on how Indians had taken over our value systems and destroyed them while watching our favourite (Indian) stars on the small remote-less TV. Daadi never could resist tapping her feet to the Bollywood songs, smiling away behind the muslin dupatta that she held to her face.

The label "South Asian" can pretend to be as inclusive as it wants to be—South Asia, however, does not allow difference. It's a blanket word that often smothers. Being Pakistani these days is far more complicated than just being South Asian. Being Pakistani can sometimes also mean "suicidal bomb-exploding Muslim extremist with ties to Al-Qaeda or ISIS," so even though I would instinctively want to assert my Pakistani-ness in conversations—because being non-Indian is the root of my identity—I have learned to be slightly calculating about it, watching the tide of the conversation carefully, waiting to see if being Pakistani is a good thing or a bad thing on that particular day.

I am well aware of the fact that when people—and here I refer to parents at school grounds during drop-off and pickup, service personnel at stores and restaurants, etc.—look at me (if they look at me) they see an Indian first, and either call me Shanti (by default, because all Indian women are called Shanti) or say "namaste," proud of their own cultural sensitivity and inclusivity. It doesn't happen every day, but often enough to remain on my "watchout" radar every time I choose an outfit to go out, or each time I walk into a salon to get my hair cut. Should I wear the "kurti" with my jeans, or should I go with the striped T-shirt from Old Navy? Wearing the kurti with jeans places me in a neat little niche of ethnic womanhood and a striped T-shirt signals assimilation, but then, it's not Muslim enough. Should I get my hair cut short, or should I keep it long? Short hair, dark skin claims to Pakistani strangers that I may not be from Pakistan, but long hair and kurti can show that I'm trying to hang on to Pakistani rules of modesty (and fashion) while trying to assimilate—so what image do I want to project today?

And to think, I haven't had breakfast yet.

That brings me to being Muslim and then Pakistani. Or is it the other way around? I have yet to decide whether I am Pakistani before Muslim or vice versa. Part of my conundrum is that while Pakistan's foundation was laid on the idea that Muslims could not, would not, live alongside Hindus in a Hindu-dominated India, Pakistanis' interpretation of what it means to be Muslim differs from the Middle East's definitions—and that the Pakistan I thought I knew has changed, and from this distance, it feels as if the Pakistan of the 2020s wants to be very much like Middle Eastern Muslim-dominated countries. Many Pakistani Muslims still revel in the cultural freedoms of being South Asian, while trying desperately to fit in somehow with their more "pious" Middle Eastern counterparts by donning the hijab, but keeping the dupatta with the kameez-shalwar. These nuances play out dramatically in Canadian mosques, where Pakistani women will be the ones wearing traditional kameez-shalwar to prayers coupled with matching hijabs covering hair instead of the dupattas. There is no other place better than diasporic settings to highlight regional differences in religious norms and traditions—but it is also diasporic settings that seem to be working hard to erase those nuances.

Bring immigration pains, motherhood, and academia into this mix and you've got an inkling of the identity soup I've been struggling to name.

Most academics—including myself—maintain an ideal image in their heads of teaching during the day and spending our evenings at home. But those who are raising children while also fighting to maintain precarious footholds in the academic world know that it does not always work this way. The ones who succeed are those with strong support networks in place, with grandparents and (expensive) nannies and babysitters constantly available, or spouses who take on the bulk of the child-rearing and household-management work.

The academic workday never ends and nor does mothering, meaning academic pursuits involve an intensely difficult juggling act. Some of my professors, in an effort to be helpful, have recommended the pomodoro technique—work in one-hour time slots, complete with egg timers. When the egg timer goes off, switch gears, play with the children for the allotted one hour, then return to work—be it research, lecture-planning, or marking papers. But that only works if your children are old enough to entertain themselves for the one hour you are supposedly working, and if you yourself are adept at the kind of code-switching required by this technique. When you have really young children without grandparents within driving distance, you are in deep trouble. Family life can become complicated very quickly, and most organizations and institutions—including academia—do not have any systems in place that can help with those complications.

I moved from Pakistan to Canada with my husband and our three-month-old baby. By the time I began my doctoral studies, my daughter was eighteen months old and my husband (who arrived with a master's in sales, and a fifteen-year career in a high-profile, multinational company) was still struggling to find a stable, well-paying job. He was taking on minimum-wage jobs to keep our family afloat, which meant rotating shifts and an inflexible schedule with no vacations or sick days. With no family around, I relied heavily on babysitting services, which meant I never had enough money for anything else. I could not afford to buy books, or sometimes even groceries.

When my daughter was around three years old and I was preparing for my comprehensive exams, I became pregnant. It was joyful news—a celebrated, wanted pregnancy. I was a teaching assistant at the time, in my second year of my doctoral studies, assisting a Canadian Studies specialist in an introductory course on Canadian literature.

When the professor found out my news, he told me that he *could* make a comment to me about people like me, rabbits, and breeding, but that he would not actually say it.

By that time, I had completed four years of undergrad, and two years of graduate studies in Canadian universities. I had heard the full gamut of comments on my accent, the quality of my vocabulary, my confidence, my exoticness. His comment stayed with me but did not surprise me. I told myself then that I should be grateful that he thought enough of me to stop himself from actually making the joke, and that once I got that great tenure-track job, or published that best-seller, I would show him that I was more than just a brown baby-breeding machine.

My pregnancy became complicated in what felt like the blink of an eye. My sixteen-week ultrasound was scheduled in the same month I was to complete my second year of my doctoral degree. I had completed three of the four requirements and needed to complete an exam that was to occur in front of an examining committee. At the ultrasound appointment, I watched the technician become increasingly agitated, and then call her supervisor in to take a look at the images of my baby. When I asked if everything was okay, they wouldn't look at me, nor would they answer my questions. My heart knew then that something was wrong, but I went to my exam anyway. I passed the oral, but my heart hadn't been in it, and I know my examiners picked up on it.

My doctor called me the day following my comprehensive—my baby had a condition called triploidy. She had an extra set of chromosomes. She was not going to survive, and I was asked to "abort" my child, while I listened to her heartbeat on the monitors, and felt her move. I was creating a baby but somehow, I had failed to create her right. It took me five weeks to agree to what the doctors and my family were advising me to do, because I knew that as long as she was inside me, I could protect her, keep her safe, keep her alive.

I ultimately agreed because I realized I would not have any support or help if I decided to try to carry my baby to full term, give birth to a child with birth defects (provided she survived the pregnancy and birth), and then spend an unknown amount of time waiting for her to die.

The choice—to keep my child or to "abort" her—actually felt like a non-choice.

After the procedure, my marriage ended up on the rocks, and I spiralled—but I was able to stop short of losing it all completely because of a scared little girl waiting for her mother to smile. I focused on getting by, one day at a time, trying to keep myself from losing my mind by focusing on submitting my field study proposal and beginning work on my dissertation. It took me another four years to complete the dissertation, during which time I became pregnant again and gave birth to my son. My marriage survived because we went to couples counselling; my sanity survived because I focused on a goal that, I believed, would give me validation when I achieved it.

With two young children and in the fifth—then sixth and seventh—year of a four-year program, with no funding, no jobs on the horizon, and an unfinished dissertation, I came very close to quitting multiple times, especially when I faced the prospect of putting children into babysitting, being penniless and sitting in front of my computer working on a magnum opus that remained unfinished in spite of three years' worth of reading and writing. As my supervisor so aptly put it—I was a hard worker, but my work was consistently looking for a sense of direction.

I found that direction in the seventh year, when one woman (who was not my supervisor) felt invested in my work enough to take it upon herself to help me through. She empathized, but held me accountable, and shepherded me through a system designed to weed people like me out. She encouraged me to write when I felt unable to, then sent me thoughtful feedback on my writing and gave me a sense of direction. She championed my work when my supervisor wouldn't and stood up for me at a time when no one else thought I was worth it. I owe my degree to her.

After completing my degree, I tried to hold on to multiple sessional teaching positions but could not quite get the coveted full-time tenure-track job. And after ten years of knocking (banging) on the closed gates of academia, I have finally moved on, but with a lingering sense of failure that I just can't shake off.

I have invented and reinvented myself multiple times, and looking back now, I wonder where it was that I lost the dream of becoming a writer.

When did I lose my way?

During my undergrad, I earned a coveted spot in the creative writing course and developed what was called a "promising" portfolio by my professor. I graduated with the belief that one day I would turn that portfolio into my magnum opus. Over the years, I have kept that portfolio with me, holding on to the binder through multiple moves, sometimes hiding it away, at others, pulling it out to rifle through its pages, revisiting the person I used to be.

Years later, I ran into my creative writing teacher—a published writer in his own right—after graduating with my doctoral degree. He remembered my portfolio and asked if I had published anything. I told him that I hadn't yet had the time to devote to my creative writing efforts. His response—*well, if you truly wanted to become a writer, you would've made the time*—floored me. I now wish I had had the presence of mind to introduce him to Virginia Woolf, and the very real need for a room of my own—which I still do not have.

Here I am, eight years later, the portfolio still with me, untouched but treasured.

The electronic files were lost long ago, but it's still on paper, and this year, I moved it to my desk.

Among the many hats I have worn, perhaps the most difficult one to cope with is the household-management and "wife" hat. I put "wife" in quotation marks because the term is loaded for a Pakistani Muslim woman. In as much as I would like to assert my feminist politics, I have to admit that I have internalized "wifehood" and all that it means in South Asian terms, including the part that appears to be anti-feminist—the one that can only envision a wife as the sole homemaker. I do all the cooking, the cleaning as well as the myriad other tasks that go into maintaining a busy household, while being a nurturer and friend to my husband. I keep track of all medical appointments, ensure that everyone gets where they need to be, and that the refrigerator is fully stocked at any given time.

It is funny how this is turning into a list of all that women do during a busy day, whatever "ethnicity" they embody or embrace. What makes South Asian mothering so much more complex or unique, given that almost all women in the developed world are struggling with similar issues?

I believe that the answer lies in the inner conflicts and the social pressures we face as South Asian women. I am consistently grappling with the question of cultural traditions, of religious injunctions, and the conflicts that are a result of raising children who have no real attachment to the homeland left behind, and longed for, by their parents. I was raised by a mother who believes that an ideal wife supports her husband's endeavours without questioning or undermining him; that she nurtures his dreams even at the cost of her own, and that she looks after the household and the children while he takes care of all matters related to the "outside" world. I know that these beliefs make up the fabric of my own value system.

Islam does not necessarily forbid women from working outside the home—it is not actually required of them—and this has been interpreted to mean that women should not need to work for a living. According to religious tradition, if a woman decides to work outside the home, the money she earns is hers to keep, and the husband is still financially responsible for the upkeep of the household. That has been interpreted to mean that even if a woman works for a living, her real, valued, labour is what she does inside the home for her family.[17]

In practical terms, this can become exhausting, because no matter what we do during the day, it is our responsibility to ensure that all housework is completed, and the family's comfort ensured. Thus, not only do we put in all the time and effort required to maintain our careers, we also shoulder the responsibility for the entire household, with the tacit understanding that since it is our "real" job, we should not complain, nor should we expect help from our husbands. This makes heavy demands on mental and emotional bandwidth, demands that feminists have discussed extensively in recent years.[18]

This is not to say that being a Muslim mother and a feminist is necessarily a conflicting identity. Islam values mothers highly; one tradition proclaims that the door to jannah (heaven) is located under a mother's feet, which has been interpreted to mean that loving and caring for your mother will guarantee a place in heaven. There is no comparable tradition for fathers, so not only is motherhood honoured by the religion, it is almost revered, viewed as the pinnacle of selfless love and sacrifice. South Asian traditions view motherhood in a similar way. As Vijay Mishra[19] shows, the figure of "mother" in India is not just that of a nurturer, a sustainer, or even just "mother earth," but the carrier and transmitter of "culture" (in itself a loaded word). We are all familiar with the argument that it is the mother's responsibility to "teach" and to educate the offspring, along with fulfilling the role of the nurturer. With her connections to the motherland, the subcontinent, the source of culture and religion, the South Asian immigrant mother in Canada, then, carries a heavy burden—that of transference of cultural and religious identity along with the emotional loads already discussed.

Personally, I worry about how many of these values to pass on to my own children. It is generally hard for me to fit, to belong. I wasn't sponsored by my husband; I was the spousal sponsor, which complicated the culturally prescribed gender roles we embodied in our relationship. I moved back to Pakistan when we got married, and only returned to Canada with my husband and daughter two years later because I wanted to pursue my doctoral studies.

I feel like I am no longer an outsider to Canadian society, unlike many other immigrants who migrate as adults. This means that I have a complicated relationship not only with the South Asian community, but also most Canadian mothers I meet at playgrounds. I cannot be, I don't want to be, neatly pegged into one neat identity box—as much as they need me to be.

I remain committed to my religious identity—that of Muslim motherhood, of selfless love and sacrifice. But I also recognize that my children only know Canadian values and customs, that they have had to learn to navigate their various multiplicities, and are still learning the balancing act along with me. They know they're being raised Muslim, have been taught to follow certain rules, but are also well aware of the fact that they are, and will remain, different. I can only hope that my children will learn that not fitting into any one category is actually a good thing, that you can make conscious decisions about who you want to be on any given day, and that being a nonconformist is something to be desired, not abhorred.

Being a Pakistani mother in Canada, I find myself struggling almost every day with the question of cultural roots, patriotic loyalties to the homeland left behind, and religious duty while trying to put the "in" back into "visible minority." Given my Pakistani roots, my multiplicity is messy, my career choices have been questioned, my confidence undermined. I am only now beginning to examine what a successful life looks like, realizing that the dreams I had were forgotten—perhaps set aside—when I decided to become a mother.

Having recently closed the door on my own academic aspirations, I am now raising two young children while juggling the demands of a burgeoning freelance business and a busy household. I grapple with multiple, socially predefined roles that I need to fulfill in order to be deemed successful in every aspect of my life. This means I currently have no mental space for my true passion: writing. There's just never enough time, or money, or space, or energy.

Yet while I internalize the messages that tell me I'm not worthy, I also hope to challenge them, to find the energy and the strength to show my children that resilience and recovery are habits, not just a onetime act.

My portfolio still sits on my desk, a reminder that my dream hasn't died—not yet. I flipped through it before sitting down to write this essay, and "discovered" the poem I wrote almost ten years ago, at a time when my children were both young—and was reminded that creativity expresses itself in many different ways. I may not have managed to publish that novel I have always wanted to write, but I did manage to create for them magical stories about Eid fairies who bring special gifts in secret, stories that are now treasured family lore. If I can do that, then I also know that motherhood has made it possible for me to become a stronger writer.

I am confident that one of these days, I will finally crack open that portfolio—and find a way to say all that I have been wanting to say.

The Giving Tree

ADELLE PURDHAM

> *Before it dies, a Douglas fir, half a millennium old, will send its storehouse of chemicals back down into its roots and out through its fungal partners, donating its riches to the community pool in a last will and testament. We might well call these ancient benefactors Giving Trees.*[20]
>
> —Richard Powers, *The Overstory*

My nephew's birthday is in early June, when the spring flowers of my in-laws' replete gardens bloom and appear in their full resplendence. I crack open the hardcover of the book Dan and I have gifted him, Shel Silverstein's *The Giving Tree*, to the first page. Dan and I are in the spring of our romance, babies, really. I feel a need to perform in front of his older sister and parents, to impress upon them that I will one day be a fantastic teacher. Look how well I read! And that I will also be an amazing mother and wife. Look how generous I am with my time! Look at how I adore children and hold their attention! When the actual time comes, there will be no doubt of my superior skills.

I open my reading with verve and zeal.

"And the boy loved the tree . . . very much. And the tree was happy." Overexaggerated smile.

Undoubtedly, my young nephew was paying close attention.

At some point, the enthusiasm in my voice might have faded. You can't help but let melancholy seep in when you read *The Giving Tree*. The boy takes what he wants and leaves the tree, who loves him, behind. The tree isn't happy until she's given everything of herself, absolutely everything, to the boy. And the boy isn't happy until he's taken away every part of the tree.

Where's the joy in that?

"And so the boy cut down her trunk and made a boat and sailed away. And the tree was happy . . . but not really."

Reading the book then, I felt a sense of indignation on behalf of the tree. Why did the boy have to be so greedy as to take it all? The tree gives everything to the boy—and for what?

It is only at the beginning of his life and nearing its end that the boy is able to appreciate the tree for her true worth: he appreciates the tree for what she is instead of what she can provide. I'm reminded of a line from Haruki Murakami's memoir, *What I Talk About When I Talk About Running*: "I don't think we should judge the value of our lives by how efficient they are." The same could be said for trees, and for humans.

I'm not sure if my nephew hung on to my every word or not. I can't even picture where the two of us were sitting as the earth outside renewed itself around us. Was he snuggled into me on the couch or sitting in the armchair across from me? Was I in the armchair while he sat on the couch? The specifics don't matter. What was important was that when I finished reading that book, I knew one thing: I never wanted to be the tree.

Over ten years later, the school day is nearly done. I tuck three mini boxes of Smarties into my coat pocket to dole out, one for each girl. I greet you with a kiss on the forehead and take your backpack from you. You hand it to me today, which is nice. Sometimes you leave it for me on the ground. Often you throw it on the ground. The wind feels rough, bitter cold. Winter whispers her frosty breath. You refuse to wear a hat or put your hood up or wear gloves. Your hands are bright pink, but you don't seem to mind. We're on our way home and it's just another day. The Smarties will keep you happy for a while.

We walk in a small cluster: me, you, your older and younger sisters. Your hands slide inside the too-long sleeves of your jacket and I hold loosely on to your sleeve in an attempt to keep our cluster moving, to keep you happy. And you are fairly happy. *Smarties!* This makes you smile and so I am smiling.

You say something, something I can't understand. I ask you to repeat, but I can't quite catch the meaning.

We approach Charlie, your favourite crossing guard, and you find your place by his side, take his hand and we safely cross the street.

Now empty, I offer to take back the Smarties box.

"Yes." You hand me the miniature cardboard container. I think this is all you need. I hope.

But, on the other side of the crosswalk, you ask again for something. Again, I do not understand you. Softly, I ask you to please repeat, but I don't stop walking, I press on. I sense things are moving in the wrong direction and, when this happens, I just want us to be home.

You don't try to explain again. You won't; instead, you start to scream.

"No! No! No!"

"Honey, honey, what's wrong?" I ask, even though I know it's because I haven't understood you. Once we've reached tears, we have moved beyond solving what is wrong. Frustration prevents words and what comes out are wails and screams.

This happens so fast, this transition from walking along the sidewalk together, smiling and eating Smarties, to you screaming and wailing, and I just want it to stop.

"Stop! Lysie." Your little sister yells at you.

Your big sister walks apart from us, way far ahead.

On the surface I remain kind, perplexed, even with the feeling of sinking dread settling in. This is an all-too familiar scenario.

The thing you tried to say, what was it?

I stop walking now and face you. Crouch down to your level. What else is there to do?

"Are you cold? Are your hands cold? Here." I pull up your hood and you wail louder.

I plead with you for a while,

"Please Elyse, stop screaming. What's wrong?"

But the words are drowned out by a flood of tears.

I change my strategy, pick up my pace. We live only five hundred metres from the school.

"Come on, Elyse, let's go home. It's cold outside. We can talk at home."

I avoid the words I usually say in this scenario: *"Daddy's at home. Let's go see Daddy."* Daddy is always the prize. Daddy gets to be the prize and I feel like the problem. He tells me she does the same thing to him, in reverse, but I think he is only trying to be nice.

I don't ask if you're hungry, either. I won't consider it now. I'm done with stopping a hundred metres from home and opening containers in the freezing cold. You can wait. Why can't you just wait? If that's what it is.

Your throat becomes unblocked long enough to say you'd like more Smarties, and now I'm annoyed, because these tears, this outrage, this emotional upset *for what*? A few more coloured pieces of chocolate?

I pick up my pace, "Come on, Elyse!" and I wonder what my neighbours must think to see my daughter with Down syndrome frequently wailing as she walks down the street with me.

They must think I'm a horrible mother, that something is terribly wrong. That I have hurt her in some way. These thoughts make me feel guilty of a crime I don't understand or didn't commit. Mothers are forever getting it wrong.

When I move away from you, closer toward home as a tactic to get you to keep moving forward, you only wail louder, and so I stop. You catch up. At one point you hit me. Your delicate blows are like wayward branches hitting the windowpane in a breeze, more an annoyance, the worry of scratched glass. You lack the physical power of the wind, but you make up for it with a storm of emotion. Your storm is like a heaving black cloud that's burst, and even though I know it's coming, there's no time to take cover before I'm soaked through.

I am swatted for my misunderstanding, for my lack of understanding, of being understood. Have I done this to you before? Your tears claw at my insides.

I think you are yelling at me for more Smarties, and finally, I've had enough.

"That is ENOUGH, Elyse. Cut it out, cut that out. Let's go, let's get home."

Somehow, by using a firm voice, I have regained the upper hand, but now I feel terrible. I have regained control by silencing you.

Your face is red now, from the wind and your tears. A thin trail of clear fluid drains from your left nostril. I move in silence, the rest of the way home, angry at you for making me the bad parent, yet again. Yet again, another day, another ordinary day, when I have walked you home in tears. Tears that seem to come and fall on a whim. Tears that I can attach no meaning to. And this hurts my feelings. Mothers have feelings, too, you know. This hurts my feelings until I am the one who wants to cry, who should be crying. Who later, will cry, alone in bed.

I try to understand you, but I feel like you don't try to understand me. I don't trust you. I don't trust that you won't burst into tears for reasons I can't explain and make me look like a bad mom who doesn't get her kid. And that is the source of my frustration, being humiliated by my own incompetence.

When you were in kindergarten, and I picked you up at the end of the day, pushing a stroller with your then baby sister in it, you would throw your bag to the ground at my feet and wail from tiredness or hunger or just because you could or, most likely, some unknown reason to me, and other parents would turn to me, visibly disturbed, because this was obviously the most upsetting for *them*, and they would ask me, "What's wrong?" What they really wanted to ask was, *how can we make her stop?*

Other times, their generosity was too much, *what can I do*? Their eyes pleaded. *Nothing, stop looking at the spectacle of us, please go away*. But I didn't really mean that. Not that I wanted to be a spectacle—I didn't; but that I can do it alone—I can't.

Sometimes I want to be like the French photographer Anna Grevenitis. Her photography appeared in *The New Yorker*, an evocative series of black-and-white photos she took of herself and her daughter with Down syndrome engaging in daily tasks together. Anna, the mother, looks directly at the camera in each shot. In one photo, she holds out her foot for her daughter who's painting her toenails while facing squarely into the lens in defiance, the tattoos and shaved head on her left side on full display.

When you are crying, I want to freeze frame, shoot the camera, with just my steely gaze staring back at onlookers. I want to dare them, with cold eyes, to even look at me or you. Sometimes I just want to hide; I don't feel like picking up children from school and disturbing the positive flow of my afternoon. Children are such unknowns.

I'm trying Elyse, I'm trying. Do you see me trying?

We burst through the door to our house and you're still wailing and now I'm anger boiling over, frustrated in my own right. Now *I* throw your backpack onto the floor.

Why do we have to do this this? Every. Single. Day. Same old shit, and I'm tired of it.

Your backpack sits askew alongside the other two backpacks belonging to your sisters, and I move past them into the kitchen to cool off. Your tears are subsiding, but I need to be away from you. I'm trying not to be angry at you for being upset, because that isn't fair. It isn't fair to be mad at someone who's hurt, but now I am hurt, too, and whose feelings matter? Do a mother's feelings count at all?

I empty someone's lunch bag, perhaps pull the yogurt container out of the fridge for snack. When I turn back around, you are sitting on the floor beside your backpack and fingering "your stick," a beloved fishing rod that belongs to a board game where fish get hooked on to the end. I had no idea the stick was tucked into your backpack. Nobody told me. Or so I thought.

You're holding the small rod in one hand and fondling the hook on the end of the string with the other, mesmerized.

"My stick. My stick."

"Elyse," I say, "you wanted your stick?"

"Yah," you say.

"Okay, then next time, instead of screaming and crying, can you please just say that. 'Mommy, I want my stick'?"

And you sit there, eyes focused on the hook, dangling, dangling. Swaying back and forth. You are calming yourself down with the hypnotizing motion.

And I think back to the walk and remember you said the word "stick." Right after we crossed the street with Charlie, right before the tears.

"I want my stick." That might have been what you said.

I was carrying it the whole time in the backpack on my shoulders.

I would have given it to you, had I known; of course, I would have given it to you.

"Sorry, Elyse. Mommy didn't know."

But I'm not feeling very sorry, and my words come out indifferent, without effect. I'm still feeling angry, hurt, betrayed. *Sorry I didn't know about your stupid fucking stick.*

I feel angry, but that feeling oscillates with a sort of knowing empathy. I can't ignore the telepathy mothers intuit in regard to their children's thoughts and emotions. You just wanted your stick, and nobody gave it to you. Your own mother wouldn't listen.

Why didn't I just stop moving for a minute more?

But it's not that simple. We have a past. I did stop moving, remember? And tears. More tears. Wails. A mother can only take so much.

I have two other children. A husband. A dog. Myself to worry about.

Ariel. She was gone. Long gone down the street. I was in no position to ask about her day. Other than telling you to stop, Penelope stayed silent. She's the one new to kindergarten who should be crying from exhaustion and hunger. The children have learned there's only room for one person's tears. It isn't always you, to be sure, but your tears stain me in a way that's hard to explain. I find it hard not to take your tears personally when I have tried so hard. Perhaps it is the trying that's the problem.

From where I'm standing in the kitchen, I can hear the dog whining in his crate from the living room. I call your dad to come upstairs from the basement, away from his work.

"I need your help," I tell him. I can't take it, this not being good at my job.

He comes upstairs and finally I can breathe. The piano teacher arrives and you are smiling again. A deep exhale, and I'm getting there too. The piano teacher passes me a loaf of bread, freshly baked from her husband, a thank-you for some editing work I carried out for him. A job I am good at. *Food!* Now I am happy again. I am like the giving tree. *But not really*.

Later that night in bed, I'm reading Richard Powers' *The Overstory* and the idea of the giving tree reappears in a new form. "People see better what looks like them," he writes, "*Giving trees* is something any generous person can understand and love."[21]

The next day, I try again. To be a good mother, that is.

I double down on my efforts. I grab three boxes of rainbow-coloured chocolates and one "stick," which I pocket.

The weather is fair today, no need for mittens. I arrive at the school and greet all three children with hugs and kisses. You pass me your backpack, gently.

"I'm going home," you say, heading off through the field that cuts to the sidewalk. Fair enough.

When I catch up to you, I offer you Smarties.

"No," you say. "I want fruit snacks."

"Hmm, well, I don't have any fruit snacks with me, but let's check your lunch bag."

The fruit snack packet, which I cut open in the corner for you before school, is empty.

"Oh, you already ate your fruit snacks."

"No, no..." There's less conviction in your voice, some confusion, no rising hysteria. You simply look as perplexed as I am.

"Do you want your stick?" Ah, the art of distraction.

"Yes!"

And we're off walking again, both of us in a good mood, past Charlie, the crossing guard, to the other side of the street and the final stretch.

You giggle most of the way home. Perhaps I overexaggerated earlier. Perhaps you get your flair for the melodramatic from me.

I use a line pilfered from your father. "Hey, chicken wing, chicken wing," and I nudge into your side with my chicken wing elbow. "How was your day, chicken wing?"

And you giggle this adorable laugh that's like the ringing of a bell, pure and true.

"No, no," you say through your giggles, "I want Daddy." You aren't laughing now, but you aren't upset either.

I nudge you again, gently, in the ribs.

"Your daddy doesn't want you." I use a fake evil voice.

And at this, you laugh and laugh at the ridiculous statement.

And then you play my game.

"Daddy doesn't want you!" you say.

"No, doesn't want you!" I counter.

"No, you!"

"No, you!"

And on this goes until your pure joy is written across my face in a warm, wide smile. I wish now that everyone in the world could see us together.

You curl your tiny fingers around my arm and we swing along that way, arm in arm, having found our common ground. Comedy. You are a comedian, after all.

When we get home, I unpack your lunch bag and there, at the bottom, are your fruit snacks that have dumped out through the hole I cut in the package in the morning.

"Elyse, your fruit snacks are all here! I'm sorry, sweetheart." My face lights up. "And you didn't cry! Thank you for not crying, Elyse, when you didn't get what you wanted. I'm sorry I didn't see them."

I squeeze her little shoulders and she shrugs it off.

No big deal.

As I finish this essay, my youngest comes into the room seeking my attention. I happen to be holding my own copy of Silverstein's *The Giving Tree* in my hands. I have been perusing its pages, considering the significance of the text.

"Can I have that book?" my youngest says, taking it from my grasp. She isn't really asking. Another line from *The Overstory* is jogged from memory: "A tree is a wonderous thing that shelters, feeds, and protects all living things. It even offers shade to the axmen who destroy it."[22]

And so it is with children who pare us down one limb at a time.

I smooth out my four-year-old daughter's curls on the crown of her head as she sits cross-legged on the floor beside me, turning the pages and studying them intently.

"That was a short read," she says, handing it back to me.

And the tree was happy.

Binaries

HARRIET ALIDA LYE

Nine months pregnant, eight days before my due date, I was feeling confident and level-headed and like part of my life's purpose had just become clear. I was offered a deal for my second book, a book I'd been wanting to write, obsessed about writing, for fifteen years. The book was a memoir about a unique and highly fatal form of leukemia that I had at the age of fifteen, exactly half my life ago. If I survived, the effects of chemotherapy, I was told, would be sterilizing. When I became pregnant unexpectedly, the book's shape suddenly made sense to me: I knew that I could write it as a mother in a way I'd been unable to as only a daughter.

But I came home from meetings with interested publishers in tears, crumpled into bed, and tried to put words to my feelings of guilt and fear.

"Am I allowed to have both?" I asked my partner, Cal.

He didn't understand. "Both what?"

"A book and a baby."

He laughed.

I felt certain that if I got a book then I would lose the baby, and that the only way to have the baby was to deny my career. This didn't feel metaphorical. I was terrified. Part of the book proposal included writing about my pregnancy and birth and my baby's early life. If I lost the baby, if I somehow jinxed things by promising the universe something and not delivering, would I also lose the book? I'd lose much more than the book, I thought: I'd lose everything.

Cal said, in his practical way that I love so much: "Mothers work. This is your job. Of course you can have both."

Of course, he was right.

"The feminism of writers who are mothers is a fetish," Jill Lepore writes, and I interpret this to mean: just do it, live your life, stop asking women writers if they have kids, or want them, why, why not, and if not now, then when. There is a perceived divide that you can either have one or the other. This binary became a belief system I didn't realize I held.

For much of my life I've felt split in two. When I was very young, and very shy, my private self and my public self felt like different people. In seventh grade, I desperately wanted to be in the school play and so forced myself to audition, but I burst into tears in the bathroom afterward, mortified at having made a spectacle of myself in front of the whole class. (I got the lead, Juliet, and my "ex-boyfriend" played Romeo: the kiss in the play was our first.)

As I grew up, I felt as though my creative self could never be the same as my professional self, as if art and commerce could never co-exist. Now that I am literally divided in two—out of me came another—the weights in the balance have changed. Before, it was writing and the rest, but now, it's all merged. Writing is life. Baby—we named him Arlo—is life.

One of the things I love so much about life with my now-two-year-old is his exploration of language. Arlo's words light up his memories, desires and emotions in a way that is illuminating, for the first time, aspects of his mind that were previously hidden from me, when basic communicating was accomplished without language. Now, when he wants me to pick him up, he says "Mummy, you want to come up and see Arlo?" as though he is kindly offering to carry me himself so that our faces can be closer together, and not begging for it to happen the other way around.

Ever since he was born, his understanding of subject and object has been collapsed, mutable, surfacing. When I smile, he smiles; when he smiles, I am his mirror. As soon as he was on the outside of me, I wanted always to be near him, touching him, watching him, but now I wonder whether that might have also been an intuition of what I thought he needed. For nine months we had been living in the same body. Acclimating to distance took time for us both. In infancy, mother is baby, baby is everything, everything is everything.

These days, I wonder what his private time is like inside of his mind. I tried to explain what thoughts are when he asked. (He has a book about a cat called Mog, whose aunt Posy "thinks a lot." He touched the page, pawing the cat's face that looks off dreamily into the middle distance, and said in a way that was both assertive and investigational, "Arlo drinks a lot.") He's right: thinking does sound like drinking. Drinking is an easy one, but how to explain thinking? Thoughts are like feelings, I say, but is that true? Maybe this: thoughts are the things you say without saying any words.

The first real food that my son ate, and by "real," I mean it came from a store and not my body, was plain Greek yogurt, because it's what we had in the fridge when his doctor said we should give it a try. Arlo had been alive for 163 days and sat in his high chair—which I insisted we buy months before he was born just so it was ready for this moment—for the first time. A friend, over for dinner, was tasked with taking a video; my partner Cal and I sat out of frame on either side of the baby. I held a teaspoon full of yogurt and Arlo was caught off guard when I succeeded in getting a glob in his mouth, and he looked not just confused but betrayed. Though his main goal in life was to put everything in his mouth, once *I* put something in his mouth, he didn't know what to do. What was he thinking?

"He doesn't know to close his mouth or to swallow," my friend laughed behind the camera. Breastfeeding is a closed-loop system, and babies' reflex to swallow is the consequence of the suckle.

But the next instant, Arlo's eyes lit up. He looked at the spoon again and opened his mouth. A baby bird. This was the first time he communicated with me with a language other than smiles, laughter, or tears. *More please*, he was saying, *put that in my mouth again*. I complied. His little tongue stuck out and explored the feelings and tastes of this new substance. He lunged toward the spoon and held my hands, which held the spoon, and he smiled as he tried to figure out how to get what he wanted: for the food to be in his body.

Food is the thing that takes up most of my parenting time. Every day there are three meals, three snacks; every week there's the making of the grocery list, meal planning, researching recipes that include secret vegetables, shopping, prepping, eating, cleaning, so much cleaning. This was a surprise to me.

Food has always been my mother's way of loving me. I imagine the time she spent cooking as an act of devotion, even of prayer. One of my first memories is of my mother stirring a big batch of leek and potato soup over the stove, adding a ham hock and a *bouquet garni*. I came up to her hip, she wore a thick canvas apron, and the kitchen smelled of thyme and bacon. In Wicca, the cauldron represents the womb, fertility. When I was nearing my due date with Arlo, my mother spent weeks cooking meals in huge batches for us to keep in our freezer. Nourishing her grandchild through nourishing her daughter. From mother to mother, from baby to baby; in loving my son I am reminded of the chain of love that I come from.

When I was a baby and video cameras were newfangled and expensive, my parents used to rent one. Because they'd only have the gadget for the day, just an ordinary day, all that early footage is of me doing ordinary things. When I was a teenager seeing these videos, I thought it was so odd that my parents had recorded minutes of me sitting in the high chair and smashing Cheerios into my mouth with stubby little baby hands, quietly gumming them, and smiling to myself. Me sitting in my baby swing by the window, little stockinged legs wiggling happily, the sun shining brightly through the slatted white blinds.

But now, on my phone, I have dozens of videos of Arlo doing the same: shovelling pasta shells into his mouth, holding a peach with both hands and sucking the juice like it's lifeblood, eating ground beef as if it's popcorn while our two dogs are at his feet, learning to love him as they eat his crumbs. It fills me with peace to watch him take pleasure in meeting his needs.

Arlo eating real food also feels, in some way, like a metaphor for the collapsing of previously held boundaries: something foreign to his body is turning into the molecules that make his body grow.

Just as everything is everything, everything feeds everything else. Arlo was once foreign to me, the concept of motherhood a vast unknown, and now, because it is my life, it is also my work. My second book, a memoir, talks about Arlo coming into this world, and my third, a novel, an idea I've been percolating for years, catalyzed in my mind when I added a child.

Motherhood gives me new colours to paint with, new feelings and experiences I've never had before. Love—both a thought and a feeling—has so many new shades now: love as wanting-to-eat-your-whole-tiny-body, love as insomnia, love as never wanting to be apart from you, not knowing how you are.

Fear is a manifestation of love; this is also new to me. The experience of being so happy you're afraid of losing that happiness was familiar to me, and motherhood feels like that but exaggerated. I check on him every night to make sure that he's breathing. Because I love him so much, I worry more.

There's a new kind of grief, too—it's anticipatory, dreading when the time comes that I can't kiss his whole body, when his face doesn't light up when I come into a room, as though I am the only light he needs. In these ways, too, I am split in two: the new brightest love comes with its most profound darkness.

Here, I know, I can have both. I am learning that there can be two sides to something where one aspect does not exclude the other but rather accepts it, integrates it, and sometimes, perhaps, lies dormant for a while, but never disappears.

What Have You Done Today?

KELLEE NGAN

One of the few pieces of parenting advice I follow is to have regular family dinners. Over twenty years of research confirms that kids who eat—and talk—with their parents tend to have better nutrition and higher grades. Stronger vocabularies and self-esteem, too. It's akin to therapy with a buffet option, which is the kind of two-for-one deal that should appeal to every multitasking mother out there.

To get the conversation started around our dinner table, we play a game. It's a game in name only, but it does the trick. We get buy-in from our kids and avoid the typical response of "nothing" when we ask them to share what they did at school that day.

The premise is simple: somebody asks, "What have you done today?" and somebody else provides a summary of their day's notable activities and accomplishments. Easy. There are no points awarded, but sibling rivalry inevitably rears its head. They'll find a way to keep score, from who goes first to who talks the longest. They also like to point out if a certain story has already been shared on the walk home, which is a violation of the nonexistent rules.

My kids both love winning, so they give it their best effort. What works in their favour is that everything is a big deal for them. Even the most mundane activities are communicated with verve and delight: *I went to the bathroom—by myself! We used scissors—to cut tissue paper!* On top of that, there are so many childhood experiences that are indisputably life-altering. Take the kindergartener learning to read and write—it's impossible to undersell the news that you are actively becoming literate.

Reading practice is part of my little guy's after-school routine. We'll sit on the couch with his home reading kit—a pamphlet-sized reader toted in a worn Ziploc baggie—and dive into the day's selection. I'll read it aloud first. He'll scan the words and illustrations as we go, running his fingers over the pages, committing as much to memory as possible. When I finish, he'll take the reader from me and say, "Now I'm going to tell you a story, Mama."

He does an admirable job for a newbie. He rattles off the words he knows and guesses at the rest with such assurance that I'm almost convinced of a printing error on the page. Recently, I offered praise when he recognized "together"—both a ten-dollar word in his realm and winning fodder for dinner conversation. His response, however, was a nonchalant mic drop. "It has a lot of letters, sure," he said. One page later, he encountered "together" again as if it were drawn in hieroglyphs, mumbled a mangled approximation, and shrugged all the same.

I have to admire his confidence. Some days the words flow with ease; on others, progress requires the painful extraction of every thought and letter. Yet he's never fussed whether he struggles or succeeds. He's just happy to be doing it. He'll keep bringing books home in that well-worn plastic bag and fake it until he makes it, never doubting the ultimate outcome.

Their father champions participation overachievement. Every night he's the one doling out high fives between servings of rice, cheerleading our reports with over-the-top enthusiasm. And he's not above quoting motivational cat posters as encouragement, either. He's quick to offer a "Hang in there!" if ever self-doubt creeps into a retelling, forever stressing the impossibility of losing at this game.

But there are moments when it feels as if losing is exactly what happens, especially when it's time for my turn.

"Mom, what have you done today?"

The short answer, especially on a weekday, is that I worked. On a typical day that means I wrote a lot of emails and attended a lot of Zoom meetings. Interspersed with these work-from-home hours are the hours of working for our household: the laundry, the cleaning, the cooking of the sacred family meal. There are also the school runs, piano lessons, and homework to be marshalled. A bill to pay. Or a sock that must be found before the five-year-old can go on living.

But who cares? This is not the stuff of Christmas letters or social media posts but the material of my daily load: working and parenting, both the doing and the worrying about.

And then, there's writing: my quietly persistent artistic practice that, like a younger or undersized sibling, can struggle to keep up with the big kids. Writing will sit to the side and wait, resigned to being picked last from my never-ending to-do list.

But it remains on the roster, always hopeful to get into the game.

It was during a recent creative streak that I'd reported what I thought was a victory for myself and my novel-in-progress.

"I wrote five hundred words today," I'd said. There was an implied "*ta-da!*" as punctuation but everyone failed to pick up on it.

"Is that a lot?" the kindergartner asked. This is a kid who used to spend hours being charmed by mismatched Tupperware lids. Now that he's in school, he's got opinions and is far less easy to impress.

His sister interjected. A third grader, she is turbo-charged on reading and will burn through a novel in one sitting. She will gladly tell anyone who asks that she *gets* books. And math. I could see her doing the addition in her head, fingers tapping on the table to double-check the calculation.

"But aren't there, like, millions of words in a book?" she said. The upspeak at the end both the result of two missing front teeth and a desire to be at least a tiny bit diplomatic.

"It's more like tens of thousands," I said. But neither of them was particularly interested in the distinction. Five hundred out of any larger number equals not enough.

My kids are harsh but fair critics, something I attribute to their genetic heritage. My parents would react the exact same way, viewing the typing of five hundred words into a computer document as inconsequential until proven otherwise. It's not that they're unsupportive; it's that they have no time for flattery. Praise from my parents is delivered in the same matter-of-fact manner as a takeaway order. When I texted my mother to ask for her opinion on the episodic children's audio play I'd worked on, she replied: *Listened to two, so far, should be good for the kids.* Then she e-transferred Lunar New Year lucky money with instructions to buy her grandchildren something they could use, like pants.

My mother and father arrived in Toronto in the late 1960s from Jamaica and Hong Kong, respectively. They met at the Chinese Catholic church they both attended and would go on to star in their own version of the immigrant success story in which their stoic work ethic led to a better life for themselves and their Canadian-born offspring.

When I was young, I recall that my parents worked a lot. They both had full-time jobs. My mother was a teacher at a community college, my father an electrician. For a period of time my father worked night shifts, his career path diverting from normal waking hours. His schedule rendered family dinners impossible some days, but there was always food on the table.

Their dedication to their work paid off. My father eventually switched his focus to real estate, another career with great time demands but better returns. By working hard—and never quitting until they were offered the golden handshake of early retirement—they were able to buy a house, put me and my older brother in a variety of activities, and neared the apex of Asian parenting by sending us both to university.

What I don't recall is them doing much for themselves. They'd chauffeur us to school and our extracurriculars, but they rarely bought new clothes or went on vacations as a couple. They take yoga and tai chi classes now as empty nesters, but I don't think they did anything like that before: No pickup soccer for old-timers, no wine night with friends. If they went to the rec centre, it was to take one of us kids to swimming or soccer or skating, and the nearest thing to a night out would be a family wedding—with the emphasis on family.

In the rear-view mirror, the sense of duty and sacrifice flashes to the point of blinding.

Starting in pregnancy, mothers begin to lose parts of themselves.

In a 2018 *New York Times* article entitled "Reframing 'Mommy Brain,'" writer and doctor Alexandra Sacks refers to a study by pediatrician and psychoanalyst Donald Winnicott that explains the phenomenon known as primary maternal preoccupation. Dr. Winnicott found that mothers, out of necessity, must laser-focus on their helpless dependent in order to keep said dependent alive. Our grey matter shrinks, our brains altered to narrow our focus to our children.

While this psychological state of intense attentiveness is necessary to help the baby thrive, it can come at the detriment to the mother's psychological well-being. If the baby is her world, what happens to everything outside of that orbit? What becomes of those parts of that woman that existed before motherhood and are independent of her identity as a parent? Talk about a no-win situation, where tending to your own needs is seen as a dereliction of duty.

The culture of contemporary motherhood has tried to rally against this imperative. In recent years, the messaging has been that mothers can—and should demand to—have it all. "All," in these instances, meant killing it at the mom game while climbing the corporate ladder. From the stories of working mothers "leaning in" à la Sheryl Sandberg, to the rise of mommy influencers who've parlayed parenting into a paid gig, examples of successful motherhood have remained centred on the reconfiguration and rebalancing of work and family.

The math seems faulty, or at least, incomplete. It supposes that it only takes two parts to make the whole mother: her career and her children. It supposes that our interior lives are less notable and in no need of nurturing. Why can't mothers strive to have a fulfilling social, spiritual, or creative life, too? To not only care for loved ones, but for ourselves?

Of course, there are mothers whose creative practice is their work. And full-time art moms are my heroes. I applaud them, respect them, and not-so-secretly envy them. That's the dream: to do what you love and get paid for it. That dream, however, is tempered by the reality that art is not often well compensated. According to a 2018 study by the Writers' Union of Canada, more than 85 percent of writers earn an income from their writing that is below the poverty line. If the majority of working writers in this country can't support themselves through writing alone, how can one hope to support a family?

A good mother provides security for her children—this is the tale I've been told. The moral of the immigrant success story makes it clear that I should focus on feeding my children food over poetry. Five hundred words a day will not keep them alive the way a steady paycheque will. Five hundred words a day won't pay for opportunities.

I've been reminded of this advice often. After ferrying me to university for the first time, my parents went to the campus store to buy a tchotchke to mark the occasion. I thought they'd pick something with utility like a mug or a mouse pad. But they opted for a flimsy bumper sticker that looked like it had been printed from a glitchy dorm-room printer. It read: MY MONEY AND MY DAUGHTER GO TO CORNELL. I remember them having a good chuckle about it, saying, "It's funny because it's true."

They never put it on their car. Instead, it was tacked above the clothes dryer in the mudroom of our house where, when I returned on breaks, I'd be guaranteed to see it and be reminded of their sacrifice—and that the least I could do is help with the laundry.

Before I had kids, I vowed that I wouldn't let motherhood change me. But the babies came along and they wreaked their havoc. Not just on my body, but my brain. Thanks to that change in grey matter, I now spend a disproportionate amount of time feeling bad about what I'm *not* doing.

This guilt occurs regularly, most often expressed in a stream of consciousness downward spiral that my husband refers to as my homage to Lucy Ellmann's *Ducks, Newburyport:* The fact that I can't be a good writer if I don't dedicate more time to it, the fact that I don't have time before my board meeting, the fact that the kids need to finish their Valentine's Day cards, the fact that no one will want to publish my book even if I finish it—I probably won't finish it; the fact that the roast won't defrost in time, the fact that I forgot take the roast out of the freezer, the fact that I don't have enough time to write, the fact that I can't write when I have time, and the clock in the kitchen has stopped.

"Why do I even bother?" is the standard coda. My husband waits for me to utter this closing line before he responds in his usual rational fashion: "You wouldn't feel so guilty about it if you didn't want to do it."

That much is true: the need to write persists, as does the desire to be a good mother. The solitary exercise of writing has always appealed to my introversion: the opportunity to be alone, but also in a world of my own making. It's a lot like tackling a jigsaw puzzle. Both can be an exercise in frustration, given the inevitable stalls in progress and hours spent staring at the holes in the scenes. But as a mother juggling a mental laundry list of tasks and the burden of emotional labour, there's no greater feeling than figuring out how all the pieces fit together. To know that my brain still has space to make sense of chaos and, for that moment, to control it.

My husband is sympathetic to my cause and will offer to morph into his parenting superhero alter ego, Fun Dad, and get the kids out of my hair for a few hours. The kids love this arrangement because they know they're going to get treats. No mission with Fun Dad is complete without a stop for ice cream or McDonald's drive-thru, and this is after going swimming or sledding or horseback riding or whatever delightful activity he fabs up that day. Fun Dad's superpower is Big-Time Childhood Memory-Making.

Fun Dad will text photos to me while they're away, practically live-Tweeting what they're doing without me so that I won't feel left out. I'll type various heart emojis in reply while the regret takes hold. He'll ask how the writing is going and that's when I'll send a thumbs up even if I've spent most of the time doing a deep dive on YouTube cooking videos.

Among the most instructive is a series where a chef attempts to cook a three-course meal using random tools and devices. Watching this woman wrestle with frying blini on a hair straightener can only help to inform how my protagonist might deal with similar adversity. Because what if said protagonist was lost in the woods and needed to melt chocolate buttons on her cellphone battery to survive? I'd have to know the MacGyver-style mechanics to make the scene believable, right? I have to do the research, so I have to watch the videos. Besides, I don't even own a flatiron.

When the three of them return home and we gather for a meal and a debrief, I'll brace myself for impact.

"What've you done today?" I'll ask my kids, even though I have a sneaking suspicion of what their answer will be. They'll say that they've had THE BEST DAY EVER! and Fun Dad's reign as favourite parent remains secure for another day.

The family dinner is supposed to boost the spirit and health of everyone involved—not just the kids, but the adults, as well. But in these moments, any writing accomplishment is undone and all I feel is guilt. Writing guilt and mothering guilt; that gnawing reminder that when you've made time for one thing, you've forsaken the other.

Five hundred words a day may not keep my children alive, but the attempt to make those words count helps keep me going. Writing is a reprieve from my obligations when I'm not someone's mother or colleague or spouse; a moment to unspool some bit of story from the periphery of my grey matter and bring that part of myself back into view.

Would I love to publish a bestselling book and win a bunch of literary prizes? Of course, but that endgame is hardly a consideration. For now, writing time is borrowed time. So, when the kids are tucked in their beds or I have a lull between meetings or laundry cycles, I'll sit at the little desk in our office and try to write. The desk is usually cluttered with the ephemera of this life: the puzzle pieces and coffee cups, permission slips and spreadsheets; a lucky cat waving its golden arm, hopeful and steadfast. In the corner sits a miniature cactus that seems squishier and sadder than it should be. I should probably send it to the compost heap, but I'm a sucker for the visual allegory. Like writing, it will bloom again under the right conditions. Just give it some light and time and good things might happen.

Five hundred words a day will add up. They'll form sentences that form scenes that will grow into chapters. Then, eventually, there will be a completed manuscript—accompanied by the feeling of relief and the smallest allowance of pride. I won't know what will become of the novel, if it will make its way out into the world. All I'll know is that I made it to the finish line. And I'll claim this as a victory, however fleeting.

I'm already looking forward to that dinner when it happens. And who knows, with a little more time and little less YouTube, it could be soon. The four of us will be seated around the table, eating and playing our game. Someone will ask me what I've accomplished that day and I'll finally have something momentous to report.

I can imagine their reactions now. My daughter will request to read the book. Fun Dad will throw a high five my way and propose a toast. And my son, ever the pragmatist, will stare at me with a straight face and say: "Okay, so, what are you going to do now?"

FOUR

SELF

Echolalia

ANONYMOUS

Today, I ripped a piece of tape and held it out on my pointer finger. You took it without looking and stuck it on the jar. I ripped the tape. I gave it to you. You took it from my finger. You stuck it on the jar. I ripped the tape. I gave it. You took it. You stuck it. I ripped. I gave. You took. You stuck. Me to you. You to me. We went on like this for an hour. Me to you and you to me and me to you. Our fingers touched like needles casting a stitch.

Driving home last week, you said "oh" and I said "oh" and you said "oh" and I said "oh" and you said "oh" and I growled "oh" and you growled "oh" and I sang "oh" and you sang "oh" and I whispered "oh" and you whispered "oh" and I laughed "oh" and you laughed "oh." Until I had you, I skipped right over "oh." But now I think of it constantly.

"Echolalia," says the pediatrician, but all I hear is "oh."

I got you out of the car seat. We admired how the "oh" shifted in tone between the underground parking lot and the elevator. Oh. Oh. Oh? Oh? Oh! Oh!

A noise startled you, so I lifted you up. As the elevator lurched, you put your hands on my cheeks as I said "oh." Maybe you wanted to feel the way the word left me, how my muscles worked to say it. Oh, oh, oh, oh. You pat-pat-patted my cheeks: your eyes elsewhere. Then, you put your forehead against mine, studying me up close.

As we arrived on our floor, you rested your head on my shoulder. "Oh," I said, trying to spark the exchange again, but the game was finished. You sighed into my collarbone.

When I was a child, I hid under my bed and recited *The Phantom of the Opera* from beginning to end for hours. No one sang along. Given how I wore out that tape, my family had to work hard not to learn the lyrics.

"Why don't you go out and recite that for the seagulls on the carport roof," my grandma would suggest, after half an hour of listening to me to try sing all the different characters' overlapping voices in the imbroglio section of "Notes/Prima Donna" by myself.

I played with Barbies for too long. I turned to fiction because no one would talk to me in a way I understood. In writing, I could control each side of the conversation. I could braid my loops and tangents and misunderstandings and fragments into a narrative arc. I could set my too-muchness between quotation marks, writing and rewriting until someone wanted to hear it.

When I told my mom that I was getting you assessed for autism, she said, "Oh, those doctors don't know what they're talking about. They said you were autistic and look how you turned out."

I had long suspected, but never knew. In naming you, I named us both.

Since having you, I've lost my capacity for narrative. All my stories fall out of their containers, unwieldy. I'm left with these long sentences: and then and then and then. I repeat myself. Maybe it's fatigue. You don't sleep well. Maybe it's hard to write my own words when my head is always filled with *Daniel Tiger's Neighborhood* songs.

You can't answer a question, but you can memorize an entire song or book after hearing it once. You have a *Daniel Tiger's Neighborhood* song for every situation; your language is a mix tape.

You bring me a toy, singing a song about taking care of each other, and I sing it back.

You put on your shirt, singing a song about the pride of solving a problem by yourself, and I sing it back.

I said you can't answer a question, but maybe that's wrong. You can't answer a question that ends with a question mark, but there are lots of ways to ask questions.

When I watch you gather stones at the beach, I collect information: the tilt of your head, how your breathing changes when you're about to get upset, the way you delight in the wet sand between your fist but hate when your hands get dirty. Your hands answer questions. Your breath answers questions. The stones you choose answer questions. They are not always the questions I ask.

When I do write, I find myself writing to you and about you. I start writing to you and end up writing to myself. I slip into second person so easily.

I have become One of Those Moms I got warned about before I had kids: one of those moms without her own stories, who writes about her kid, who talks about her kid on Twitter. But I want to sing you out loud. So few people get to know you, my love, and you are so fun to know.

And so I share glimpses of you online. Sometimes I feel I should stop. You can't give consent. Does the anecdote belong to me or you or do we pass it between ourselves?

When I talk about you online, I don't say the word autism, because that's your story to tell. I would never talk about the hard parts: just your joy, your cleverness, your intuition. Often I think people don't believe the stories I tell about you.

"Three-year-olds don't have that kind of attention span," another mother once told me after I showed her a picture of the tape on the jar. "It must have just felt like you were doing it for an hour." Even when I'm telling the truth, people read it as fiction.

Once, you wanted to take your pink blanket to daycare, but it was dirty.

"Mom, where's my pink blanket?" you asked: beginning a scene from Daniel Tiger when Daniel's red sweater is in the wash, swapping "red sweater" for "pink blanket."

"It was dirty, so I washed it," I said, leaping into the role of Mom Tiger. I would rather be Mom Tiger—a perfect mom who was developed by a team of child psychologists working for PBS and Fred Rogers Productions to model positive parenting—than be myself.

We went through the whole scene word for word: swapping "red sweater" for "pink blanket." In the end, you took a different blanket to school happily, both of us singing.

Look how I turned out.

I was interviewing a potential care provider for you and told her about the tape on the jar. She offered strategies to move you out of fixation, to redirect you away from solitary play.

"I don't think it was solitary," I said.

"She needs to learn that it's okay to spend time in her world, but she needs to spend time in our world as well," she said gently. I was not sure who the "our" was referring to, since I always seem to be floating just outside of that word.

Since your diagnosis, I am supposed to sort through various acronyms (ABA, ESDM, Self-Reg, RDI, SLP, OT, BI, BC) pick an approach, recruit "care providers" and assemble them into your "care team." By "care" I mean intervention. By "care providers," I mean that we must identify "areas of concern," and hire government-approved professionals who will observe you and write care plan reports with measurable goals, which will be passed on to other professionals (speech, behaviour, occupational therapy) to execute. Your personality must be sorted into bullet points, action items.

"Child displays elopement," one provider notes, by which she means that sometimes when we are at the park you will be crouched down turning a pebble over and over in your hands, and then without warning will take off running, not looking back or slowing even as I run behind shouting your name, shouting "Freeze!," shouting "Red light!," since we have been practicing freeze tag and red light/green light at home, and it would be so beautiful to see you practically in flight, shedding your hat and mittens as you run, except that we live near busy streets and once a stranger had to grab you as you ran into traffic and once two crows saved your life by swooping down to caw at you, and I cannot rely on the grace of animals or strangers to keep you safe, so we just don't go to that park anymore. Is the area of concern the street or the running girl? The running girl or the mother who does not understand what propels her daughter forward, what connection the girl sees between the pebble in her hands and the sudden urge to move and keep moving?

I mention the tape on the jar in another interview.

"That's called emotional knitting," the provider says. "You're calming her nervous system by doing a repetitive task with her over and over."

"It did feel like knitting," I say, not sure if I should be comforted that we're intuitively doing a calming thing, or sad that even our moments of togetherness have a clinical name.

I posted photos of the jar with the tape online. People called it beautiful, praising your eye for detail.

How much of our creativity is misunderstood as compulsion?

Today, you said "a cake of soap" and I said "a cake of soap" and you said "a cake of soap" and I said "a cake of soap" and you said "a cake of soap" and I said "a cake of soap" and I know I am supposed to be redirecting you.

Look how I turned out.

I am writing to you, or I am writing past you to myself. I write fragments and I need someone to take them off my finger and stick them into an order that fits.

I don't think you completed me. I was whole, just strange. It's more of a shock of recognition: of liking some obscure band and finally meeting someone who says, "I love that song."

When I'm uncertain, I turn to books. Since your diagnosis, I've been reading about autistic rhetorics. I read a manifesto by Sophia Maier, V. Jo Hsu, Christina V. Cedillo and M. Remi Yergeau about fractals as a rhetorical pattern, which begins, "You already know what we are talking about. We are talking about the experience of finding it impossible to fit in. No matter how you shape yourself, you are always further confined by infinitely regressive borders."[23] I'm drawn to the second person, which feels as if someone is welcoming me to join them. I don't understand much of the article, but it's soothing to turn the words over and over, looking for patterns.

Maybe my writing is falling into fractals these days: repeating, multiplying, resisting narrative borders. Maybe it's not about productivity or brain space, but about giving myself permission to delight in my brain's loops and digressions. Maybe I am less stuck and more becoming.

I honed my storytelling abilities because I couldn't sleep. I couldn't sleep because I was afraid. The only way to direct my brain away from fear and toward sleep was to tell myself elaborate bedtime stories featuring my blue pig stuffy Sid and my teddy bear Timmy. I'd begin the story in the same spot and repeat it from memory, adding a little each time, removing elements that didn't soothe me. How much of my compulsion was mistaken for creativity?

The manifesto talks about the "commitment to the program of disorderly survival—surviving as oneself by carving out spaces for oneself-in-community."[24] I have the disorderly part covered. Not sure about the survival.

Maybe I am just annoying everyone.

Look how I turned out. I grew up thinking every child studied other kids on the playground and rehearsed how to play house correctly; I just wasn't practising hard enough. I figured other children also found tags and sock seams excruciating, but they were just better at powering through and not complaining. I had a constellation of misunderstandings but no way to connect them. I just needed to be better, to work harder, to pay closer attention, to power through, to keep powering through. My mom used to say, "If you had brains, you'd be dangerous." My mom used to say, "When they called out for brains, you thought they said trains, and you didn't want to go anywhere in life."

What interventions would I have wanted? The knowledge that my struggles had a name? For someone to teach me how to play house or have a sleepover?

I interview provider after provider. They mostly feel like sales pitches: act now! The window of intervention time is closing! She's so young. She still has a chance at a good outcome! They tell me about past clients who were like my daughter, using the phrase, "But now, you can't tell there's anything wrong.... Well, not *wrong*," they correct themselves. "But you just can't tell she's, you know... that there's anything..." They share testimonials where parents speak of "unwrapping" their children, and finding the "real child" underneath. My love, you are not some Christmas present. No piece is missing from you.

I repeat the phrase: "I am not interested in moving her toward typicality. I am interested in reducing her frustration and anxiety."

I repeat the phrase: "I am not interested in moving her toward typicality. I am interested in reducing her frustration and anxiety."

I repeat the phrase: "I am not interested in moving her toward typicality. I am interested in reducing her frustration and anxiety."

I repeat the phrase: "I am not interested in moving her toward typicality. I am interested in reducing her frustration and anxiety."

My love, I will resist turning you into a story.
My love, they will never capture you in progress reports.
My love, we won't bend to narrative arcs.
My love, I will sing you a chorus.

Lite-Brite Times Square

HEATHER O'NEILL

There was something about having a baby at twenty that made me wake up from childhood with an abruptness none of my friends experienced. It was like having a cold glass of water thrown in my face. I was all alone, with no help from my family or the father's family. I had to figure out how to support myself and the little baby I had named Arizona. I did not want to be on welfare like the rest of my family was, because then I would be a third-generation welfare case. If you grow up on welfare, you know how hard it is to get off.

I went to meetings for young single mothers in the upstairs of a church. I sat in a circle of folding chairs around a pile of donated clothes we were allowed to root through while the guest speaker lectured about birth control, or locating a baby daddy, or how allowing illegal activity in your apartment might result in you losing custody of your child. One day a woman lectured to us about the dangers of being on welfare.

"It is a proven fact that once a person is on welfare for five years, they will almost never get off," she said, looking around the circle to see whether her words were sinking in. The young mothers pulled on the cords of their hoodies, pulled out compacts and applied makeup, or nodded off from exhaustion.

I felt a surge of horror flood through me. I knew empirically that those words were true. I was going to do something with my life. Not only for myself, but for my daughter, too.

I was raised during the eighties when child psychology took a sudden shift and regarded events that happened in a child's upbringing as responsible for their later characters. A cover story in a 1983 *TIME* magazine called "What Do Babies Know?" by Otto Friedrich stated:

> The current discoveries about how much a baby sees and hears and knows at the very moment of birth make the parental responsibility seem even more formidable. Most important, in a way, is that these findings are changing the way people actually see their own children, changing how they talk to them, what they expect of them.

Any faults an individual might have were attributed to events in their childhood. There were articles that said your baby's personality is fully formed by the time they are three years old. And there's nothing you can do about it afterward. This was very alarming news. Imagine the consequences of every minute action. Were an orange to roll off the table and land on her head, she might hate Florida. If you played heavy metal at breakfast, a child might grow up and always wear their bangs in their eyes. Say you allowed a barking dog too close to your baby's stroller—they could grow up to be a verbally abusive boss.

I would have to give her a wonderful childhood if I wanted her to be a wonderful person.

But part of her having an incredible destiny meant that I had to have one myself. Wasn't it true that in order to ensure a happy childhood for a little girl, her mother would have to be happy and successful herself? It seemed obvious to me that it was.

I decided I would be a writer.

The one thing about my life that made me believe I was destined for more was that I wanted to be a writer. My writing had always set me apart in some way. It was the only thing I remember teachers in elementary school and high school praising me for. I had a small shelf of dinky trophies I had won from short story contests that meant the world to me. I had a pin for having the top grades in English at my high school that I liked to wear on my leather jacket. It was the only thing in the world I could imagine doing that would make me happy.

I spoke to a social worker about educational programs for young single mothers like myself, with the baby reaching for the pen on the counter.

"I would like to study to be a writer," I said.

"A writer?"

"Yes, like novels and poems and such things."

"Oh, no, no," the social worker said from behind the glass partition. "I'm so sorry. But you can't choose to be a writer. Here is a list of options you can choose, though."

He slid me the pamphlet underneath the glass, looking genuinely sorry for spoiling my dreams. I didn't even look at the pamphlet's list of jobs. I was too intent on being a writer.

Never mind school, then, I thought. *I'll go right into the field.*

I worked on freelance gigs, copy editing, anything. Then I wrote a screenplay that was produced by the CBC, much to everyone's, including my own, surprise. It was about a teenage girl who wanders around Montreal with a suitcase, doing drugs and sleeping on the sidewalk.

The film garnered very mixed reviews, but it was the beginning of a theme I wanted to develop. And, more importantly, it gave me a paycheque that allowed me to take some time off to work on a novel.

There is nothing more isolating than staying home with a baby. I lived in the cheapest, most rundown apartments in the city. I could never call the landlord if there was something wrong with my apartment. If they did repairs, they would raise my rent and I wouldn't be able to live there anymore. I once experienced a moment of Beckett-like absurdity when I found myself holding an umbrella over my head as I had my morning pee to protect myself from the water dripping from the ceiling. I later fixed the hole with duct tape.

I could not work at home. Instead, I would set off to the library. I was quite adamant about carrying a briefcase around with me in those days. I thought it made me look like a professional. I hoped it might make people consider me differently, although it probably didn't. I was in my midtwenties and wore extravagant suits from Goodwill and pleather high-heeled boots. I wore my hair in a ponytail on my head, and regularly passed for a teenager and my daughter's older sister. Much of the time, I had to bring my daughter along to the library with me. Arizona also had a briefcase of sorts. She had a large plastic tool box with a bright red handle that she would fill with art supplies. We both headed off with our briefcases in tow.

Being in the library requires a certain level of decorum and quiet. In the adult section of the library, the patrons arrived generally by themselves. They communicated with no one. They found themselves a chair and remained huddled over their newspaper or book or tax forms for hours. If they did something as human as nodding off, they would be kicked out immediately.

Arizona and I were able to be quiet, but we lacked decorum. The children's section was a little more lenient when it came to rules. A child would be splayed on the floor staring at the ceiling with their mittens and boots lying around them as though they were pieces of them that had broken off. There were children playing Battleship. There would be a child sitting in a chair shaped like a giant hand, reading up on the increasingly absurdly horrific circumstances of orphans while eating a box of Goldfish crackers. There would be a child who was so indecisive about which *Asterix* comic he was going to check out that he seemed quite mad. So we would set up in the children's section of the library. It was unclear which world I was a part of anyway, that of adults, or that of children. I felt very much like a teenager who was exceptionally mature for their age.

I would take out my notebook and pens. I would also have a binder filled with inspirational prompts for the novel I was working on. I would cut out photographs from fashion and art magazines, ones that captured the strange, daydreamy, insouciant look of people on the margins, ones who translated the hidden beauty of that world.

I wanted to translate what was beautiful about my life, in an attempt to prove my humanity in a novel—in a metaphorical language—despite the fact that everyone around me seemed hell-bent on telling me I was a pathetic loser who was contributing to the world being an ugly place. People wanted to equate me with graffiti written on the wall of a decrepit building, whereas I wanted to see myself as a small bird painted on the wall in Versailles.

Arizona had very different skills than I did. She was extremely crafty. She would take out her sketchbook and markers and begin making drawings of frogs who wore bowties and burped out thought bubbles filled with odd statements, replete with grammatical errors and spelling mistakes. "Healp me mother. It is not I am frog!"

The writing of a novel takes several years, and as she became older, she would take out felt and sewing needles and thread and make extraordinary donkeys. Other children at the library would regularly come to see whatever project Arizona was working on. They would stand as near to her as possible, leaning forward on their tiptoes. They wouldn't speak to her. They regarded her as a master engaged in her craft and they knew better than to disturb her.

They were not at all interested in what I was doing. There is very little that is objectively interesting about a writer scribbling in a notebook. From the outside it looks as though you are engaged in the same activity, year after year.

When we got home from the library, we would read the books we had taken out together. Arizona loved being read to. I loved children's books, too. This was a good arrangement because that was about all I liked to do in the house. She handed me paperback novels and we would lie in bed and read them from cover to cover.

I had gone to school to study literature which, more or less, means learning to read in a critical, thoughtful, engaged way. I was a master reader. I could tear through philosophical texts while riding on the subway. Before I had my daughter, my evening reading consisted of writers like Georges Bataille, Simone de Beauvoir, Jean Genet, Roland Barthes, Marguerite Duras, Wole Soyinka, Frantz Fanon, and Angela Davis.

Once a critical reader, always a critical reader. Now I found myself doing close readings of texts by Maurice Sendak, Roald Dahl, Ludwig Bemelmans, Beatrix Potter, and Astrid Lindgren. We went through the histories of giraffes with height complexes, bears who suffered from depression, mice who were tired of their feet.

The contrast in reading material was such a strange juxtaposition that I found it inevitably infected my writing with a syntactical preponderance for childlike phrasing and absurdity. There was now something in my writing style that was a cross between Jean Genet and Dr. Seuss. It encompassed both the lurid sexual desires of adult outsiders and the awkward pronouncements of curious children for whom all words are new and have multiple meanings. It brought to my writing a joyful idiosyncrasy and playful transgression I'm sure might not have existed there otherwise.

It is so hard to balance having a child with doing anything. You have to look for every free moment you can. If I waited to have alone time, it would never come. I didn't only write that novel in the library. I wrote whenever my daughter was playing or distracted or engaged in something else. I wrote that novel everywhere.

I wrote at a plastic table under a red-and-white-striped sun umbrella at the amusement park. I wrote on a bench in the zoo next to a tiger who carefully imagined me lying in a giant hot dog bun with relish on my head. I wrote in the playroom of a McDonald's. I wrote in the cafeteria of an Ikea. I wrote on a long-stained chesterfield at the Salvation Army. I wrote in the corridors of a ballet studio with skinny ballerinas going to and fro. I wrote at the cafeteria in the museum while eating a small slice of lemon pie balanced on a plate. I wrote at intermission during a play about a clown who was depressed and did everything on roller skates. (It is hard to wash dishes with roller skates, let alone take a bath or put pants on. But it is very, very beautiful. Hence, his depression.)

I wrote in notebooks and was in desperate need of a computer. I met a single mother who was running a scam. (Single mothers, you can't trust any of them!) She said the government was giving single mothers who earned under a certain income $800 to buy a computer. She told me she knew a guy who worked in a computer store. He would give me a receipt for a computer and I would give him a hundred dollars, while keeping $700 from the government.

I was very pleased at this proposition. But I did not want to scam the government. I wanted to take advantage of this opportunity. I asked the computer store guy for the information and paperwork, and took them home to fill out and send to the government. When I did receive the voucher in the mail, I was thrilled. Naturally, I took it to another computer store. I didn't trust the scammer to sell me a computer. I might buy a computer from the scammer, take the box home and open it, only to find a Lite-Brite toy in there.

My friend's brother gave me a lift home from the store with the computer in the trunk. I typed and typed and typed. I gave up everything I had once believed would characterize my twenties. I gave up on travelling. I gave up on getting more schooling. I gave up on the idea of living in New York City. I gave up on being a fixture on the club scene. I gave up on having fabulous boyfriends who were mad about me. I definitely gave up on having a husband. Instead, I typed and typed and typed.

Then one day the computer blew up. The monitor made a banging noise as though it had just been shot. And smoke began to escape from it.

I decided the novel was done.

I was now going to try and get it published. I had gone into credit card debt to finish writing it. If I did not sell it, I had no idea what I was going to do. I would be completely ruined and destitute. I was turning thirty. I had banked everything on having a successful novel. This was, of course, the most hare-brained money-making scheme. Being a single mother working on a novel is like asking a clairvoyant to book a ticket on the *Titanic*. No, no, no, it's a bad idea. But when you have a calling, you have a calling. There's nothing you can do except listen to it.

I was wary about the cost of printing the novel at the copy store. I decided to get it printed while I was in the CBC building, recording a story. The second floor was empty except for one producer. He was hunched over his computer. "Go and distract him," I told my daughter.

Arizona turned immediately and went down the hallway. She stood inside the door of his office, as though that were a perfectly natural thing to do. And she began chatting adorably with him.

I had a floppy disk in my pocket. I went into an empty office. I slid the disk into the console, pulled the file up on the screen and pressed Print. I closed the file, got off the computer, slipped out of the office and hurried over to the printer, which had already begun spitting out pages. I kept saying, "Come on, come on, come on," to the printer.

At that point something rather dire happened. The producer Arizona was talking to decided to print something as well. He poked his head out of the office, and saw I was in queue for a printing job, so he went back into his office and continued chatting with Arizona.

"What is your mother doing," he asked. "Printing a novel?"

"Yes," Arizona answered. "As a matter of fact, she is."

"What? Really?" he said.

I started scrambling to pull the last pages of the novel out of the printer. I shoved the manuscript in my oversized briefcase and slung it over my shoulder. I walked down the hallway, took Arizona by the hand, waved at the producer, and headed down the hallway. We picked up our pace and didn't stop until we had pushed through the heavy CBC doors.

I was now out on René Lévesque Boulevard. The sun was down. We walked through the sordid little Montreal streets around the area. It was filled with homeless people and drug addicts holding out their paper coffee cups for change and their pieces of cardboard on which they had written their sales pitches in magic marker. Some claimed to need the money for things like their children or their dogs. Others claimed they were saving up for an evening hamburger or a bus ride back to Nova Scotia. Their demands were so small.

What was it that saved me from that fate? Was it the baby, having to straighten out my life, so that I couldn't continue the self-destructive spiral that would have led me to sitting on the curb with a sign in my hand, an unpublishable poem on it in Magic Marker? Or was it my desire to write that made me crystallize everything into one goal?

This book had been a Northern Light that I was following this whole time. I had been in such a desperate lost place with no direction, I had looked to it as though it were the North Star. Any action that diverged from that star, I avoided.

Perhaps it was a combination of the two.

We turned onto Ste-Catherine Street, in what is known as the Gay Village. The streets were lit up in a million colours, shining from the different restaurants and nightclubs. People sat at tables drinking wine and eating and laughing. It made it seem as though everyone were bathing in the glow of a Christmas tree, in the living room of a perfect family. A family in which you really felt included. A family in which you felt as though you belonged.

I walked with Arizona under all the colours of the rainbow. And we had indeed finally found our pot of gold. I had a novel in my purse. Now I just had to find a way to sell it.

I had written a few essays for an editor who ran an online magazine in Canada. He then took a job at *The New York Times Magazine*. He had told me one of the editors he worked with was married to a literary agent. Here was my chance! I would pass my book to this editor, who would give it to his colleague, who would then give it to her husband...the agent! The agent would love it and ask me for a meeting. It was still an era when it seemed normal to do things in person. I had heard you had to network. That was how proper adults did things.

So the next week I bought two Greyhound bus tickets to New York City. That was where people went to be artists and have their dreams come true. I knew this from Kermit the Frog's Muppet movies. He was the only one of the few male figures in my life who was decent. Even his foibles and flaws were decent. My life would have been so much better if only I had met a man like Kermit the Frog.

On the bus ride, I pulled out my manuscript. I had forgotten to print the numbers on the bottom corners of the pages. I handed it to Arizona and gave her a pencil to write the numbers. "I got this!" she said. When I looked over several minutes later, she was at 203. When I looked over several minutes after that, she was at 147. Well, who was to say page numbers had to be chronological? Weren't they in large part decorative? I hoped no one would notice. (Reader, they would.)

As with everything I did, it had to also be an activity for Arizona. This was because she needed to have a wonderful childhood. She needed to be exposed to the world and culture so she would grow up lovely. When we got to New York I was so excited for her to see Times Square. I had gone to New York City with her dad when I was nineteen years old. I had always thought Montreal was such a big giant city filled with the most beautiful nightlife and signs. But I was in no way prepared for Times Square. I had just stood there blinking at it. I felt like I was a fetus that had just been born and was squinting at the hospital room and its mother's face, totally bewildered that the world could be so much more enormous than they thought.

I thought I could experience it all again through Arizona's eyes. I tied a blindfold over her face when the bus became stuck in traffic driving into the city. She sat there next to me in the enforced darkness. When the bus reached its destination, I took her hand in my one hand and the suitcase in the other. She stayed very close to my body as I navigated the bustling bodies that were all around us. Some people moved out of our way when they noticed this odd couple, but it was New York so most people didn't pay us any mind. I yelled at Arizona that we were going up a flight of stairs. And then once we were outside, I didn't have to say anything. The air was filled with so much noise, honking, footsteps, construction, voices. Then when we were in a spot on the sidewalk in the middle of Times Square, I pulled off her blindfold and yelled, "Behold!"

Arizona stood there, her eyes wide open, looking around, in obvious awe. She did not say anything for a moment and instead she just looked and looked. She looked so incredibly small. And isn't that how we all feel: tiny in the face of wonder? And yet in the enormity of the world and all its billions of people and its infinity of windows and doors and things, we had our own people to whom we are the most important thing, and who are the most important thing to us. Arizona and I were already the main characters in each other's lives. But now we went to see whether I could be of relevance in anyone else's.

After we dropped the book off at the *New York Times* building, a few blocks away, we stood next to each other in the elevator going down, rather nervous.

"We've been writing this book forever," Arizona said. "I feel like we've been working on it my whole life."

I found it funny that Arizona spoke of the book as something we had collaborated on. But when I reflected on it, I realized she was not wrong. She had been my constant companion, always physically nearby when I was writing, and the ideas and imagination of people who surround you, for better or worse, affect the tenor and composition of your inner narratives. Whereas I might have wished for fellow intellectuals, I instead had a very little girl. She had forced me to write in playgrounds and zoos and had odd speculations. And weren't her illustrations and felt donkeys influence for the tender, broken, vulnerable world I was creating in the book, which I had called *Lullabies for Little Criminals*?

"I know. But let's not think about it anymore for a while. I don't want to sit on a bench and worry about it. Let's go see the sights!"

We went to Coney Island. We went to the freak show and watched a woman with tattoos all over her face eat live insects out of glass jars. We went to the American Museum of Natural History and saw walls covered in butterflies and a replica of a whale so big it looked as though it had swallowed the ocean from a water fountain and was now worried about the consequences of spitting it out. We went to the Strand bookstore and spent the entire afternoon wandering farther and farther away from each other in the stacks and then finding each other as though we were both looking for opposite paths through a labyrinth.

We stayed at different friends' apartments. One day, we went to the Tenement Museum where they showed the type of apartment a family had to live in at the turn of the century. As the guide lectured on the tight confined space of the oppressive apartment, Arizona and I turned to each other and shrugged. We would have taken the apartment in a second, if we could ever afford such a glamorous space.

Afterward, we walked on the Bowery together. I told Arizona about how this was a famous street, noted for its historical abundance of hobos. I was pulling my suitcase and was dressed in an American Apparel dress that was really just a long undershirt. I had once tried to dress more conservatively. But I had looked awkward. Like a criminal at a murder trial who was wearing a suit for the first time in their life. So, instead, I wore what I felt pretty in.

A man lying on a bench looked up at me passing and said, "That's a beautiful dress." *Well*, I thought, *if man who has been so damaged by the world that he is lying on a bench notices that I am beautiful, so must everyone else*. It put a skip in my step.

We walked to Washington Square Park. Arizona immediately ran toward the playground, hoping to make some friends. I went to the pay phone to make some calls. I called my friend Starlee. She told me an agent had been calling around looking for me. The whole time I had been wandering around the city, he had been looking for me! I took down his number and called him. He asked where I was and when I told him the park, he told me to wait, that he'd be right over.

I changed in the phone booth. Just like I was Superman. Finally! I was a position where I was called on to use my superpowers in the outside world. Instead of going around in my bumbling, inept, inappropriate role of mother, I now had to switch into my writer persona. I had a cheap pinstriped suit rolled up like a danish at the bottom of the suitcase. I had brought this along in case such an occasion might arise. I shook it out. It was made of synthetic material, so I didn't have to worry about any wrinkles.

I pulled the suitcase into the playground and gave it to Arizona.

"Keep your eye on this," I said. "I'm going over there to meet the agent."

"Okay!" she said.

I went to find a bench in plain view, a little ways from the playground. I sat there waiting. I looked over to Arizona. She was on the other side of the gate, watching, and she gave me a thumbs-up. I winked back.

Down the Middle

ALISON PICK

I am packing for Beijing. My daughter is two, and sick, with bright red circles on her cheeks and a river of snot coming from her nose. I am part of a support group for new mothers, and the facilitator is always encouraging us to "share the hardest part." The hardest part now is that I'm about to leave my daughter. The hardest part is that she doesn't understand.

When my daughter is born, I've already been writing for a decade and have three books to my name. But the year she turns one, I publish a novel that gets nominated for a big prize. This means many things, but chief among them is that my daughter's formative years will be comprised of an endless series of difficult decisions that I must make: whether to say yes to writing or to mothering. Whether to stay or to go.

The hotel in Beijing is incredibly fancy. My bedroom has a huge free-standing bathtub in front of a wall of windows, and a bed that a whole family could sleep in. I calculate the time difference in order to Skype back to Toronto. On the other side of the world, my daughter sits on her father's lap wearing her fuzzy purple footie sleeper, her eyes wide and glassy with illness. She blinks into the screen, incredulous. "Mama?" she asks. "Dat Mama?"

I start to say yes, it's me, I'm here, but she holds her tiny hands up toward me. "Mama," she says. "Pick me up!"

Silence.

Her father jumps in to distract, to console. Still, from across so much time and space, I can tell my girl thinks I am *choosing* not to gather her into my arms. I watch her defences kick in. She reaches for the laptop and slams it shut.

What am I doing in Beijing?

This moment soon comes to seem emblematic of the choices I will be privileged to make for the next two, five, ten years of our lives. It *is* a privilege. I have a beautiful, healthy child. I have published books, and have invitations to promote them. I'm the luckiest woman alive. But the feeling in my body is like I am being physically torn down the middle.

When I'm three months pregnant I'm invited to teach at the Banff Centre the following October. My daughter is due in August. Banff needs to know now. Which makes sense.

Still, it is like trying to peer through a dense curtain of fog into a future that is so close in chronological time but so far from anything I've experienced. Will I be able to teach with a newborn? Is there life in outer space? I have no way of knowing and no way to find out.

I try asking other writers, women who are maybe ten years older than me and have children. "Yes!" one tells me. "Infants just sleep! And they're so portable at that age."

I can hear her school-aged kids screaming in the background, the sound of something heavy crashing to the floor.

"Newborns are so easy!" she tells me hysterically.

Others aren't so sure. Writer Lisa Moore, whose work I adore, tells me she wouldn't recommend traveling with a tiny infant to teach. Even if I'm technically able, I might not want to, she says.

When October rolls around—after I've said no to the gig—I note the date on the calendar; that this week, today, is when I would have started teaching. My breasts are bright red, my nipples infected. I have been wearing the same pair of "Ma-jamas" for two straight months. I can barely write my own name. I would no more have been able to comment intelligently on someone else's writing than I'm able to solve string theory.

I think of Lisa's careful words. I remember her telling me, gently, no.

The following October, I pack up for Banff. Now I have my year-old daughter in tow, and my mother, who is willing to help me out. I am paying for my mother's flight, so my meagre salary will be almost cancelled out. But I like to teach, and I like Banff, and deep down I feel I can't afford to decline the job, if not in financial terms, then in career ones. I don't want the reputation of someone who refuses invitations. And I'm clinging to my writerly self for dear life.

The program director at Banff is one of the kindest people in the world. He helps me secure a larger bedroom, where I pull the mattress onto the floor so my daughter and I can co-sleep. He shows me the cloakroom in the corner of the dining hall where the heavy wooden high chairs are kept. I am desperately grateful to him, as though he has made an allowance for something unfathomably inconvenient, as though he has done me a massive favour by hiring me. No part of me thinks that the fact I'm a mother is of benefit. It does not, for one second, occur to me that I have something extra to contribute.

I have talked to the writer Annabel Lyon in advance, who performed the same feat several years earlier—her own small child, her own mother. Annabel cautions me that she was pulled aside and told, gently, that they needed to see her more at meals. The dining hall is for eating, yes, but also for students to have the chance to socialize with faculty informally, which is part of what they are paying for. Fair.

At each meal, before joining the writers, I extract the heavy high chair from the cloakroom and set my daughter up. She smears her face with food and then demands to be lifted down, toddling around the buffet with my mother trailing a few feet behind her like her plainclothes security detail. She grabs people's cutlery and throws it on the floor while I try to ignore her and to come up with insightful, humorous anecdotes about publishing to share with the students. They are so gracious. They coo at my daughter, entertain her while I eat. In truth, I am incredibly grateful for the chance to analyze line breaks instead of breastfeeding.

At the end of each meal, my mother whisks my daughter off to let me work. As they leave the dining hall, my sweet girl reaches her tiny arms back toward me. "Mama!" she calls. "Pick me up!"

The Banff gig goes well—if "well" means fourteen days of being ripped down the centre.

Eight years earlier, I was a student in the program I'm now teaching in. Among our group of emerging writers was a handful of mothers, perhaps five of them. One of them confessed to me, sheepishly, that they were gathering regularly in somebody's bedroom to talk about their children. While the rest of us were playing wild games of spin the bottle until all hours of the morning, the mothers were secretly looking at photos of each other's kids, and calling home to hear about school and soccer practice. I remember I couldn't comprehend why they would do this. Didn't they want a *break* from their children? Didn't they deserve one?

I spend the next year of my daughter's life expressing breast milk into hotel sinks. I read in Ireland, in Istanbul, the Czech Republic. I travel to California and to London. I've been waiting for these opportunities, and although I wouldn't quite say I enjoy them—I am both too introverted and too sleep-deprived—I'm incredibly happy to have published a book that has found readers. My allegiance is to the work itself, and my daughter has a wonderful father with whom she bonds while I'm away. So it's not that I regret accepting the invitations. Not quite. It's that accepting them feels compromised. I'm never able to sink into them fully.

Well, isn't that life? the angel on my other shoulder asks. *Isn't life a series of compromises between what's good for us and what's good for someone else?*

Maybe. But this compromise feels interior. It's a battle between what I want and what I want. It's a war between myself and myself.

There was, and still is, a constant calculus happening in my head. Of course the financial one is the most obvious. How many books do I have to sell at a reading to pay for child care? How many people need to tell someone else about my book to make the whole thing make sense? But also, how much gain do I need in order to compensate for my daughter's loss? *Is* it a loss for her when I'm gone? I pretend I don't know the answer, but deep down, I know.

Sometime in my daughter's early years, I recall entering the hospitality suite at the big literary festival in my hometown of Toronto and seeing the writer Kathleen Winter with her daughter Juliette. I knew them from when I lived in Newfoundland. Juliette was nine, or she was twelve, or fourteen—she was some undefined age that I recognized through my haze of exhaustion only as "not a baby." Kathleen, it appeared, had reached the elusive place that I could not even yet dream of, where she could easily bring her daughter along to book events. The two parts of her life, as a mother and as a writer, had joined. Like the soft plates of an infant's skull eventually knitting themselves together, Kathleen's life—I imagined—was finally fused.

And yet. As my own daughter slowly inched her way toward this mythical age, I watched with growing horror as a new set of problems emerged. Did my daughter *want* to be in a room full of adults discussing their contracts and their agents? Was I able to fully inhabit my writerly self with my daughter beside me? What did the festival organizers think of her being there? When was my girl old enough to stay alone in a hotel room for a few hours watching TV? And, the most pressing question of all: had I somehow damaged her with all my years of indecision?

When I asked Kathleen, she was resolute. She said how good it is for kids—girls especially—to see their mothers prioritize their work, and, by extension, themselves. I clung to this like a drowning person during the years when I travelled so much with my books. Only now, looking back, do I recognize it as a prized statement that Kathleen herself may also have clung to. Not, of course, that it wasn't true. But only that it wasn't the whole picture.

When my daughter was tiny, I looked not just to writers but to books themselves to tell me how to solve this unsolvable dilemma. There was a dark memoir about the mind-numbing exhaustion and mundanity of being at home with a baby. About the sacrifice required. *A Life's Work*, by Rachel Cusk. We new mothers whispered about it, by turns praising its virtues or cautioning each other against it. Everyone had a strong opinion. Why? Because Cusk dared to tell the truth.

Years later, I am on a jury that nominates Cusk for a big award. She comes to Canada for the ceremony with her daughter as her date. The daughter is now a teenager. I cannot stop looking at her—at the black-tie dinner, at the fancy hotel bar after the ceremony. Has

Rachel Cusk's daughter read the infamous book? How does she feel about being the subject of such a scathing account? In truth, I know that Cusk had two children in rapid succession whom she amalgamated into a single baby for the purposes of her memoir. I know, having written a memoir myself, the impossibility of translating "the truth" onto the page. But still, I can't tear my eyes off her daughter. What is it like for her to know that her own existence as an infant caused her mother so much pain?

Of course—as with Kathleen Winter—this is just my projection. Maybe Kathleen never had any doubts about prioritizing her writing. For all I know, Rachel Cusk's daughter is thrilled to have been part of her mother's success. But I can only see through my own eyes, can only ask my own questions. And the question I have is about justification. Is all of this worth it?

A decade later, I have no more clarity. I expected to look back and think, if only I'd stayed home with my baby more! Or, if only I'd prioritized my writing more! But neither one feels entirely true. Or, more accurately, they both do. I want, in equal measure, to have been the very *best* writer and the very *best* mother I was able to be. I refuse the concept of "good enough" made popular by the loathsome Donald Winnicott. What does a man know of the pressure on a mother?

Recently I did a residency at MacDowell, a heavenly artist retreat in New Hampshire. I had my own studio with a fireplace and a gourmet picnic lunch delivered to my door every day. Never have I felt more nurtured as a writer.

After dinner one evening, a young actress approached me. It was American Thanksgiving, and we'd all been drinking, and now there was raucous singing around the piano in the great hall—one of the artists was a composer for Broadway. The young actress pulled me aside. I had seen her sizzle reel—she'd had small parts on several hit shows. She was talented, and beautiful, and at the age where she could no longer avoid the question. Should she have a child? she asked, not in those words, but her meaning clear nonetheless.

She asked with a hesitation I remembered. She both wanted and did not want my answer.

I told her what I always say, that becoming a mother lent my writing an urgency it didn't have before. That if she is drawn to the idea even remotely, the love for one's child is something I would not want her to miss out on. And that, paradoxically, having a child takes the pressure off art in a way that is healthy and helpful. When my career takes an unhappy turn now, as all careers do, it is so good to have something else I am equally—or more—passionate about.

Hearing myself speak, I found myself convinced by my own argument. Yes, by all means! Have a child! It was truly the best decision I ever made! But what I didn't tell the actress is that the struggle doesn't end. That even now, with an almost-twelve-year-old, I am constantly weighing her need for my presence, and my own desire for the pleasure of *her* company, with the equally pressing need for solitude and long hours of work.

I don't tell the actress the part about being ripped down the middle.

As a preteen, my daughter is relatively used to me being gone, and now she is sometimes even the one who leaves. When she does, she says goodbye so easily. There is no more holding her arms up, no plaintive requests for her mama. "Bye!" she calls. "Love you!" And walks out without looking back. It always shatters me. That part also has not gotten easier.

What I *can* see more clearly in retrospect is the unfairness of the dilemma. When I had a baby, the war felt like it was contained entirely inside me, but of course the parameters were really much bigger. I was, and still am, struggling against the rigid concept of the nuclear family, against the deeply entrenched sexism that makes mothers feel like we have to be perfect. Against a culture that gives almost no support to women artists, no allowance for the conditions that are uniquely ours. It was too much to fight against, too depressing and overwhelming, so I internalized it and reframed it as within my control: the struggle was personal. If only I could find the right balance.

Now, from here, I see a second set of questions. What if the burden did not fall so squarely on mothers? What if we valued women's art the same way we value men's? What if we paid them equally? What if the first question asked of us was not how we balance our art with motherhood?

Even now, this very minute, writing this paragraph, I am torn. I hear my daughter get out of the shower, and call me. When she was small, I would wrap her up "like a burrito" after her bath, and by some miracle she sometimes still wants me to do it. But I also want to write. Morning is my best time. My brain, in an hour from now, won't be as clear. The words will be harder to access.

I go into the bathroom where she is warm and pink from her shower. For a moment I remember how she looked when she was born. But now there is hairspray on the counter, and hairbrushes—several of them—and she is peering into the mirror at her new ear piercings. She hands me her favourite towel and I rub her belly and her long, slick, wet hair. I pull her against me and breathe all of her in, like I did when she was first placed in my arms. My baby. The funniest, kindest, sweetest kid I ever could have dreamed of.

"Thanks, Mom," she says—the childish "Mama" long ago abandoned—and for a moment I feel her body weight soften against me. Then she straightens, and reaches for her toothbrush.

"I have to get ready," she says. "You go write!"

Never have I ever loved her more.

Untitled

LEE MARACLE

I would not refer to myself as a "good" anything, particularly not a good mom on paper or otherwise. Most women I know do not like the expectation of having to be good mothers, or good wives, especially since they're not generally the judges of these expectations.

The term "good" is not thrown in front of men as fathers. I have heard people say their father was a good man, but have not heard anyone say that their father was a good dad. It is as if they are not expected to be a good dad. Men are expected to be out and about in the world—good men, good workers, sober men, men with good manners, generous men—but I have not heard of the expectation of being a good dad.

Women are expected to be good moms, and as part of that goodness they are expected to do most of the work of child rearing, housekeeping, cooking, laundering. I have not heard of the mother who is out and about in the world and without "good mom" duties. The expectation is that working or not, out and about in the world or not, the home front is taken care of by the woman—the mom. When a father looks after his children he is babysitting, just as if he were a stranger. Women say they have to look after or watch their children or grandchildren, but I have not heard a woman use the term "babysit." Babysitting is what you do for friends.

The pressure put on women is immense, the standards not attainable. We are not entitled to be angry, or "shrill" as others say. Disappointed, or guilt-tripping as others put it. Bossy, or nagging as others frame it. The expectation is that we will cheerily accomplish our slave tasks in the same efficient, polite, and friendly way we would accomplish paid work. Men have no problem dropping coins in a machine to clean their clothes, but they will not compensate the women in their lives for putting their clothes in the washing machine.

This is so normal that we expect it of ourselves and are constantly vigilant about "getting home on time to do the chores" before our partner does. We do not just carry guilt about not doing enough, we virtually live at the guilt station where the bus awaits. We get on board and ride all day under the weight of the guilt we carry. It never seems to be enough.

I make sure none of the characters in my books are immersed in sentiments like the above. I want to create guilt-free characters, so I become one. I have become the character that I want to create. I am busy sometimes, busy thinking, seemingly doing nothing, always guilt-free and hopeful. I push back on Goliath, the colonial giant, every day, with no expectation of winning, but knowing that I like the fight. I like facing Goliath.

A friend of mine is still reading and learning from my 2014 novel *Celia's Song*. He finds it a great book, especially during the pandemic, as it focuses on Indigenous people having fought and won against an epidemic. They do not have to be proud. They do not have to commend one another or celebrate the win. They just keep rolling forward through their fractured lives, gleaning joy, interest, and engagement at every waking moment.

I am a mother. My kids called me Lee for most of my life. One of my sisters was asked why they called me Lee instead of Mom. One of my kids responded: "Mom is what she is, but Lee is who she is." I loved that she thought it more important to be who I am and for her to recognize that, than to have to refer to me as "what" I am.

A group of young men once saluted me after they learned that I was Sid Bobb's mother. They asked how I managed to do such a good job raising him.

"What did you do?" they ended the salute.

"Nothing," I answered. "I just stayed out of his way."

Our story says that an elder brings us here and hangs with us until we have our feet fully on the ground—five to seven years or so. Others say, "Give me a child of three, and I will tell you what kind of human adult that child will be." In other words, it is the elder who guides the child more profoundly than anyone else. This story humbles me whenever I want to take credit for the magnificent children I have.

Get out of the way. I must be reminded every now and then to get out of the way.

My son reminded me just a day or so ago to step back. I will. My story demands that of me. We have been on this continent for thousands and thousands of years. These stories are distilled, learned from, redistilled, and retold repeatedly. There is no good mom in any of them. They are stories about clean minds, clean hearts, clean spirits, and clean bodies. Clean up your conduct is what my son asked of me. He is entitled to ask me that. It is the least I can do for anyone, including myself. But every now and then, my brain gets addled, muddies up the waters, and I say something out of turn, and my brave children stand up and push back, oh-so-courteously and with so much love, but with the thin, steely yarn that courses through them that they inherited from our people. This yarn holds them committed their freedom, their position, and their independent will.

I am not the good mom. They are the good progeny.

The notion of the good mom is the foundation of patriarchy. I pay very little attention to it.

I am a good person. I am generally as considerate as is required. If someone is not considerate to me, I presume I am not required to be considerate to them. This amounts to most North Americans.

"Most people in this country spend all their time hating us," my granddaughter said the other day and laughed as though it were a ridiculous pastime. Basically, a waste of time. I pretty much feel that way. I was also struck by the notion that not many Canadians realize how little attention we pay them. They are entitled to feel anyway they want about us, just do not use those feelings to spread ill will. We will not tolerate being mistreated by anyone.

I am a good human being. I fulfill my obligations to humanity, and I fulfill humanity's obligations to the world. I mow the grass when it is too long. I plant a garden—it is good for the earth as well as my budget. I am good to all living beings. If a spider comes in the house, I carefully carry him out without hurting him. I excuse myself when getting in the way of someone else. I do not take up more time than is my due. I have been on plenty of platforms where we are given ten minutes and everyone but me takes fifteen. I have learned to share.

My ancestors shared this country with others. Good enough. My mother shared her wealth with us, and I did with my children. Good enough. I also took my share. I am no martyr. Children do not appreciate parents who martyr themselves for their children. If my mother had done that I would not have appreciated it either. We share with one another, not equally. A small child cannot eat a steak, but no one will let them go hungry.

EDITORS' NOTE:

Lee Maracle died on November 11, 2021 in Surrey, British Columbia, prior to the completion of this collection and before she was able to title this essay. A beloved and vital figure in Indigenous literature, Maracle was known for her influential, trail-blazing career and unparalleled generosity. She was seventy-one years old.

ABOUT THE AUTHORS

ANONYMOUS has published four books, teaches writing, and lives in Vancouver. She has chosen to publish her essay anonymously because she feels her child should have control over who knows about their autism diagnosis and they're not yet old enough to make this decision.

S. LESLEY BUXTON is the author of the award-winning memoir, *One Strong Girl: Surviving the Unimaginable, a Mother's Memoir*. Her essays about loss have appeared in Hazlitt, *Reader's Digest*, *Today's Parent*, *Still Standing*, *This Magazine*, and in the Caitlin Press anthology, *Love Me True*. She is the coauthor of *Time to Wonder* with Sue Harper, the first in a series of books for children about the museums of British Columbia. She has an MFA in Creative Nonfiction from the University of King's College in Halifax, Nova Scotia. To learn more about her visit www.slesleybuxton.com.

RACHEL GIESE is an award-winning journalist and author. She is the editorial director of *Xtra*, an online magazine covering LGBTQ2S+ politics, culture, sex, relationships, and health. Her 2018 book, *Boys: What It Means to Become a Man* won the Writers' Trust of Canada Shaughnessy Cohen Prize for Political Writing.

LORRI NEILSEN GLENN's non-fiction and poetry titles include the award-winning *Following the River: Traces of Red River Women* (Wolsak and Wynn, 2017), a lyrical hybrid work exploring the lives of her Ininiwak and Métis grandmothers and their contemporaries. Glenn's poetry and non-fiction appear in numerous journals, magazines, and anthologies, and her work has been adapted for libretti. An award-winning teacher and writing coach, Glenn served as Halifax's first Indigenous poet laureate. She is professor emerita at Mount Saint Vincent University and a mentor for the University of King's College MFA program. She lives in Nova Scotia.

NIKKYA HARGROVE is an alumna of Bard College and a 2012 Lambda Literary Fellow. She has written for the *New York Times*, the *Guardian*, the *Washington Post*, *Cosmopolitan*, *Elle*, Scary Mommy, and more. Her memoir, *Mama: A Black, Queer Woman's Journey to Motherhood*, is forthcoming from Algonquin Books in Fall 2022. When she is not writing, she is working as the vice-president of Operations and Programs for a small nonprofit based in New York called Harboring Hearts. She lives in Connecticut with her family and works as a freelance writer.

JÓNÍNA KIRTON is a Red River Métis/Icelandic poet and a graduate of the Simon Fraser University's Writer's Studio, where she is their BIPOC Auntie supporting and mentoring BIPOC students. A late-blooming poet, she was sixty-one when she received the 2016 City of Vancouver's Mayor's Arts Award for an emerging artist in the Literary Arts category. Her first collection of poetry, *Page as Bone—Ink as Blood*, was released with Talonbooks in 2015. Joanne Arnott described this collection as "restorative, intimate poetry, drawing down ancestral ideas into the current moment's breath." Kirton's second collection, *An Honest Woman*, was released in 2017 with Talonbooks. It was a finalist for the Dorothy Livesay Poetry Prize. Betsy Warland had this to say about *An Honest Woman*: "Kirton picks over how she was raised familially and culturally like a crime scene." She is currently working on her third book, a poetic memoir, *Standing in a River of Time*, which will be released in 2022 with Talonbooks.

HARRIET ALIDA LYE is the author of the novel *The Honey Farm* and the memoir *Natural Killer*. Her work has been published in the *New York Times*, the *Globe & Mail*, the *National Post*, the *Happy Reader*, Hazlitt, *Vice*, Catapult, and more. She founded the literary magazine *Her Royal Majesty*, which ran for six years and republished the first-ever short story by Alice Munro. She lives in Toronto with her family.

LEE MARACLE was the author of a number of critically acclaimed works, including *Ravensong*; *Bobbi Lee, Indian Rebel*; *Daughters Are Forever*; *Celia's Song*; *I Am Woman*; *First Wives Club*; *Talking to the Diaspora*, *Memory Serves: Oratories*; and *My Conversations with Canadians*, which was a finalist for the 2018 Toronto Book Award and the First Nation Communities READ 2018–19 Award. *Hope Matters*, a poetry collection co-authored with her daughters Columpa Bobb and Tania Carter, was published in 2019. Maracle was also the co-editor of *My Home as I Remember* and served as Distinguished Visiting Scholar at the University of Toronto, the University of Waterloo, and the University of Western Washington. Maracle received the J.T. Stewart Award, the Premier's Award for Excellence in the Arts, the Blue Metropolis Festival First Peoples Prize, the Harbourfront Festival Prize, and the Anne Green Award. Maracle received an Honorary Doctor of Letters from St. Thomas University, was a recipient of the Queen's Diamond Jubilee Medal, and an Officer of the Order of Canada. In July 2019, she was announced as a finalist of the prestigious Neustadt Prize, popularly known as the American Nobel. A member of the Sto:lo Nation, Maracle passed away on November 11, 2021 in Surrey, British Columbia. She was 71.

SOFIA MOSTAGHIMI is a Toronto-based fiction writer, editor, and educator. Born in Sherbrooke, Québec, to a Québécoise mother and an Iranian father, she grew up in Mississauga, Ontario, where she mastered the art of hanging out in Tim Hortons parking lots. Her fiction has appeared in *Joyland Magazine*, *The Fiddlehead*, and *The Puritan*, among others, and has been longlisted for the Journey Prize. Her novel *Desperada* is forthcoming with Random House for Spring 2023.

KELLEE NGAN is a writer of Chinese descent and Caribbean heritage based in the traditional and unceded territories of the Musqueam, Squamish, and Tsleil-Waututh Nations. A graduate of the University of British Columbia's MFA in Creative Writing, her writing has appeared in *Geist*, *Grain*, *Witness*, *Poetry Is Dead*, *The Oddments Tray*, and *Making Room: Forty Years of Room Magazine* (Caitlin Press). She has also created and collaborated on work for live and digital performance, including *Rishi & d Douen*, an audio play for young audiences (Rumble Theatre/Carousel Theatre). Born and raised in Toronto, Ngan lives on Ne x̱wlélex̱wm/Bowen Island with her husband and two children.

HEATHER O'NEILL is a novelist, short story writer, and essayist. Her work, which includes *Lullabies for Little Criminals*, *The Girl Who Was Saturday Night*, *Daydreams of Angels*, and *The Lonely Hearts Hotel*, has been shortlisted for a Governor General's Literary Award for Fiction, the Orange Prize for Fiction, and the Scotiabank Giller Prize for two consecutive years, and has won CBC Canada Reads, the Paragraphe Hugh MacLennan Prize for Fiction, and the Danuta Gleed Award. Her novel *When We Lost Our Heads* was released in 2022.

ALISON PICK won the 2002 Bronwen Wallace Award for poetry, the 2003 National Magazine Award for poetry, and the 2005 CBC Literary Award for poetry. Her 2010 novel *Far to Go* was longlisted for the

Man Booker Prize and has been optioned for film. Pick is also the author of the memoir *Between Gods*, winner of the Jewish Book Award for non-fiction. She served on the jury for the 2015 Scotiabank Giller Prize, and has been on faculty at the Sage Hill Writing Experience, the Banff Centre for Art and Creativity, the Iceland Writers Retreat, and the Humber School for Writers. A two-time fellowship recipient at both Yaddo and MacDowell, Alison Pick lives and writes in Toronto.

ADELLE PURDHAM is a writer, speaker, and parent disability advocate. She holds an honours degree in French literature from Western University, and is a certified teacher. She completed Humber College's Correspondence Program for Creative Writing, where she wrote her memoir *Here We Are, Happy* (in progress). Her work has appeared in the *Toronto Star*, The Mighty, *Broadview Magazine*, and she's a regular contributor to *3.21: Canada's Down Syndrome Magazine*. Adelle is the founder of The Write Retreat, facilitating wellness, workshops, time, and space for women writers to create. She is currently completing her MFA in Creative Nonfiction at the University of King's College, and writing her next book, *I Don't Do Disability and Other Lies I've Told Myself*, an ensemble of first-person essays through memoir. The good mom in her loves her three kids and the bad mom in her sometimes wishes they would go away so she can write. Visit her online adellepurdham.ca.

AMBER RIAZ is a professional academic editor, and has edited manuscripts, journal articles, and conference papers, working with academic presses as well as individual authors. Since earning her doctorate in English literature, she has been a sessional instructor in London, Ontario, and in Vancouver, British Columbia. Most recently, she was the Campus Education Manager at Sprott Shaw College's

Surrey campus before being laid off due to COVID-19 in September 2020. She has taught academic writing, literature, and general education courses, in addition to offering administrative and pedagogical support to students and faculty at Sprott Shaw. Riaz has worked on the representation of mothers in film, stereotypes of Muslims in various film industries, the Partition of India, and the representation of the "burqa" in Pakistani novels. She loves working with writers, publishers, and academics, helping them find the perfect words for their manuscripts.

JAEL RICHARDSON is the author of *The Stone Thrower*, a book columnist on CBC's *q* and the founder and executive director for the Festival of Literary Diversity (FOLD) in Brampton, Ontario. Her debut novel, *Gutter Child*, became an instant bestseller in January 2021 and was shortlisted for the Amazon First Novel Award. Richardson holds an MFA in Creative Writing from the University of Guelph and lives in Brampton, Ontario.

CARRIE SNYDER is the author of three books of fiction, including *Girl Runner*, which was translated into a dozen languages and was a finalist for the Rogers Writers' Trust Prize, and *The Juliet Stories*, a finalist for the Governor General's Award. Her new novel, *Francie's Got A Gun*, will be released in 2022 with Knopf Canada. Her creative non-fiction has been published in a number of anthologies. Carrie is also the cofounder and project coordinator of The X Page: A Storytelling Workshop, a multicultural performance project that she runs in collaboration with other artists in Waterloo, Ontario, where Snyder lives with her family. You can find her on Instagram; or at carriesnyder.com, where she still insists on publishing a literary blog (her children have firmly requested she not look into TikTok).

MEAGHAN STRIMAS is the author of three collections of poetry: *Junkman's Daughter*, *A Good Time Had by All*, and *Yes or Nope*, which received the Trillium Book Award for Poetry. She is the editor of *The Selected Gwendolyn MacEwen* and the co-editor of *Another Dysfunctional Cancer Poem Anthology* (with the late Priscila Uppal). She is the program coordinator and a professor in the new Bachelor of Creative & Professional Writing degree at Humber College in Toronto and she serves as interviews editor at the *Humber Literary Review*, a magazine she cofounded. She lives with her family in Hamilton, Ontario.

JENNIFER WHITEFORD is a writer, comedian, and mother of two. She spent her teens and twenties deeply involved in zine culture, regularly publishing the critically acclaimed personal zine *Matilda*. Her first novel, *Grrrl*, a YA coming-of-age story, was published in 2006 by Gorsky Press. She writes a regular column for *Razorcake* zine, examining the overlap between parenthood and punk DIY culture. She is currently at work on a romance novel about a record collector who falls in love with a podcaster.

TERESA WONG is author of the graphic memoir *Dear Scarlet: The Story of My Postpartum Depression*, a finalist for the City of Calgary W.O. Mitchell Book Prize, and longlisted for CBC Canada Reads 2020. Her comics have appeared in *The Believer*, *The Rumpus*, *The New Yorker*, and *Event Magazine*. She teaches memoir and comics at Gotham Writers Workshop and is the 2021–22 Canadian writer-in-residence at the University of Calgary.

ERIN WUNKER is an associate professor of Canadian literature at Dalhousie University, where she co-organizes the Dalhousie Feminist Seminar Series. She is a cofounder and managing editor of

Hook & Eye: Fast Feminism, Slow Academe, and the author of *Notes from a Feminist Killjoy: Essays on Everyday Life* (Book*hug Press, 2016). Wunker is co-editor with Hannah McGregor and Julie Rak of *Refuse: CanLit in Ruins* (Book*hug Press, 2018); co-editor with Bart Vautour, Travis Mason, and Christl Verduyn of *Public Poetics: Critical Issues in Canadian Poetry and Poetics* (WLU Press, 2015); and the editor of *Barking & Biting: Selected Poetry of Sina Queyras* (LPS, 2015). With Sina Queyras and Geneviève Robichaud, Wunker is the co-editor of *Avant Desire: A Nicole Brossard Reader* (Coach House, 2020).

ABOUT THE EDITORS

STACEY MAY FOWLES is an award-winning journalist, essayist, and author of four books. Her bylines include the *Globe and Mail*, *Reader's Digest*, *Elle Canada*, *Toronto Life*, *The Walrus*, BuzzFeed, *Vice*, Hazlitt, *Quill & Quire*, and others. Her most recent book, national bestseller *Baseball Life Advice*, was published in Spring 2017, and was selected by the *Globe and Mail* and *Maisonneuve* as a best book of the year. Fowles lives in Toronto with her husband and daughter, where she is working on a children's book and her fourth novel.

JEN SOOKFONG LEE was born and raised in Vancouver's East Side, and she now lives with her son in North Burnaby. Her books include *The Conjoined*, nominated for the International Dublin Literary Award and a finalist for the Ethel Wilson Fiction Prize; *The Better Mother*, a finalist for the City of Vancouver Book Award; *The End of East*; *The Shadow List*; and *Finding Home*. Lee acquires and edits for ECW Press and cohosts the literary podcast, *Can't Lit*.

Fowles and Lee are also the recent editors of the highly successful, widely covered, groundbreaking anthology *Whatever Gets You Through: Twelve Survivors on Life After Sexual Assault* (Greystone, 2019), named a *Quill & Quire* Best Book of the Year.

ABOUT THE MOTHERS MATTER CENTRE

Mothers are at the centre of it all—families, communities, and society—and when they are thriving, everyone benefits. That is why our organization, the Mothers Matter Centre, is dedicated to serving socially isolated and low economic status mothers and their families. Our vision is to foster a Canadian society where all mothers and children can achieve their full potential and lead enriched lives. Our mission is to empower isolated, at-risk mothers by helping them develop the knowledge and capacity they need to take control of their lives and become confident parents and engaged citizens.

Our programs aim at breaking the intergenerational cycle of poverty, low literacy, and social isolation. With program variety, we can adapt to the needs of our families and meet them where they are at, as no two families are the same. The Mothers Matter Centre trains mothers to help mothers in their own homes. The trainers, or Home Visitors, all come from the same communities they are supporting. They are role models, and their most important credential is empathy. With it, they create bonds based on trust and support mothers' ability to change their own lives and their children's, for the better.

The Mother's Matter Centre's flagship program, HIPPY (Home Instruction for Parents of Preschool Youngsters), debuted over twenty years ago and has grown tremendously with over twenty-five HIPPY sites across Canada serving 1,200 refugee, immigrant, and Indigenous families.

The HIPPY program employs moms, often graduates of the program, as Home Visitors who then work with newcomer, refugee, and Aboriginal mothers in their most important role—as their child's first teacher. When paired with a Home Visitor, mothers develop their skills and gain confidence and self-esteem. The program builds bridges to the larger community, ending isolation and helping mothers take steps to prepare their kids for success in school. Home Visitors receive weekly training, employment experience, and career mentoring that supports them in their transition to other work or higher education.

> *I wasn't a fan of reading stories. So I feel really [HIPPY] was something that helped my kids and me as a young mother too. It helps me a lot to handle kids and mostly during the time of lockdown [...] I'm really happy that the HIPPY program helped me a lot on handling my kids, teaching them (mostly my son), having time with them, playing and forgetting any other thing that is going around me. Really, I felt so happy. I felt so much love to be in this country, just what HIPPY program did in my life and the life of my son and the life of my family. I really, really feel a loving and appreciate all the programs that you people are giving, and all the effort that you're putting, giving mothers. I really appreciate, and I pray that this program continues as we have seen a lot outside that they need support from the HIPPY program on bringing up the children. Thank you so much. I appreciate everything.*
>
> —Susan, HIPPY mother

Mothers are changing the world. The Mothers Matter Centre has helped transform over 40,000 lives. Mothers become more confident in their role in the family, and children are better equipped for positive early learning experiences. Be a part of the movement.

A portion of all sales of *Good Mom on Paper* will be donated to the Mothers Matter Centre, to continue the support that all mothers—creative or otherwise—need. To learn more about the Mothers Matter Centre and our suite of programs, visit our website at https://www.mothersmattercentre.ca/

Instagram: @mothersmattercentre
Twitter: @mothersmatterc
Facebook: Mothers Matter Centre
LinkedIn: Mothers Matter Centre

NOTES

1 This excerpt is from *Threading Light: Explorations in Loss and Poetry*, an out-of-print essay collection published in 2011. Copyright is with the author.

2 Lidia Yuknavitch, *The Chronology of Water* (Portland, OR: Hawthorne Books, 2011).

3 Anne Carson, "Essay on What I Think About Most," *Men in the Off Hours* (New York: Alfred A. Knopf, 2000)

4 See *The Tears of Eros*, but tread carefully.

5 Sigmund Freud, *The Uncanny*, trans. David McClintock (London: Penguin, 2003).

6 Claudia Dey, *Heartbreaker* (Toronto: HarperCollins Canada, 2018).

7 I'm thinking of Scott Frank's adaptation.

8 "Care, caring, carer. Burdened words, contested words. And yet so common in everyday life, as if care was evident, beyond particular expertise for knowledge. Most of us need care, feel care, are cared for, or encounter care, in one way or another. Care is omnipresent, even through the effects of its absence" (María Puig de la Bellacasa, *Matters of Care: Speculative Ethics in More than Human Worlds* [Minneapolis: University of Minnesota Press, 2017.

9 Sigmund Freud, "The Uncanny," trans. Alix Strachey (London: Imago, 1919).

10 Claudia Dey. *Heartbreaker* (Toronto: HarperCollins Canada, 2018).

11 Erica Jong cites this in her article "An Art Like Everything Else," and claims that Plath said this in an unaired BBC interview, https://www.nytimes.com/2004/12/12/books/review/an-art-like-everything-else.html.

12 Claudia Dey, "Mothers as Makers of Death," *The Paris Review*, August 14, 2018, https://www.theparisreview.org/blog/2018/08/14/mothers-as-makers-of-death/.

13 In *Three Steps on the Ladder of Writing*, Cixous describes truth as that which we cannot say. In *The Poetic Imperative*, Johanna Skibsrud works this into a hypothesis for poetry that understands the poem as a motile agent. I think of a swimmer, or a gull, and I like this notion.

14 Lidia Yuknavitch, "I Will Always Inhabit Water: On Living a Swimmer's Life," *LitHub* (April 2017), https://lithub.com/lidia-yuknavitch-i-will-always-inhabit-the-water/.

15 Jacques Derrida writes this several places; though I always think of it in *Archive Fever* when he reaches toward Freud.

16 This is not in fact the absolute final sentence. The essay ends with the statement, immediately following this one, that "This problem has been discussed from a psychoanalytical point of view in another place." Might this be a Freudian equivalent to *how many times do I have to tell you?* Probably not, but I find it amusing to think so.

17 For a detailed discussion of the division of labour in a Muslim household, I recommend Fatima Mernissi, *Beyond the Veil: Male-Female Dynamics in a Modern Muslim Society* (New York: Schenkum, 1975); and Sitara Khan, *A Glimpse through Purdah: Asian Women—the Myth and the Reality* (Staffordshire, UK: Trentham Books, 1999).

18 The French comic artist Emma is one of many artists and activists who have captured this division of gendered labour well. Her digital comic has been profiled in *The Guardian* (see "The Gender Wars of Household Chores: A Feminist Comic" *The Guardian*, May 26, 2017, https://www.theguardian.com/world/2017/may/26/gender-wars-household-chores-comic.

19 Vijay Mishra, "The Texts of 'Mother India,'" *Bollywood Cinema: Temples of Desire* (New York: Routledge, 2002), 61–88.

20 Richard Powers, *The Overstory* (New York: W.W. Norton, 2018), 220–21.

21 Richard Powers, *The Overstory* (New York: W.W. Norton, 2018), 220–21.

22 Richard Powers, *The Overstory* (New York: W.W. Norton, 2018), 222.

23 S. Maier et al, "GET THE FRAC IN! Or, The Fractal Many-festo: A (Trans)Crip)t," *Peitho*, Vol. 22, Issue 4, Summer 2020, https://cfshrc.org/article/get-the-frac-in-or-the-fractal-many-festo-a-transcript/.

24 Ibid., 3.

ABOUT THE ESSAIS SERIES

Drawing on the Old and Middle French definitions of *essai*, meaning first "trial" and then "attempt," and from which the English word "essay" emerges, the works in the Essais Series challenge traditional forms and styles of cultural enquiry. The Essais Series is committed to publishing works concerned with justice, equity, and diversity. It supports texts that draw on seemingly intractable questions, to ask them anew and to elaborate these questions. The books in the Essais Series are forms of vital generosity; they invite attention to a necessary reconsideration of culture, society, politics, and experience.

For more information visit bookhugpress.ca/product-category/essais-series/

Colophon

Manufactured as the first edition of
Good Mom on Paper: Writers on Creativity and Motherhood
in the spring of 2022 by Book*hug Press

Copy edited by Shannon Whibbs
Type + Design by Ingrid Paulson

Printed in Canada

bookhugpress.ca